THE AUTOBIOGRAPHY OF ASHLEY BOWEN

(1728–1813)

broadview editions
series editor: L.W. Conolly

THE AUTOBIOGRAPHY OF ASHLEY BOWEN (1728–1813)

edited by Daniel Vickers

broadview editions

Library and Archives Canada Cataloguing in Publication

Bowen, Ashley, 1728–1813.
The autobiography of Ashley Bowen, (1728–1813) / edited by Daniel Vickers.

(Broadview editions)
Includes bibliographical references.

ISBN 1-55111-781-9

1. Bowen, Ashley, 1728–1813. 2. Navigation—New England—History—18th century. 3. United States—History—Revolution, 1775–1783. 4. Québec Campaign, 1759. 5. Sailors—Massachusetts—Biography. 6. Marblehead (Mass.)—Biography. I. Vickers, Daniel, 1952– II. Title.

F74.M3B69 2006 974.4'5 C2006-902694-7

Broadview Editions

The Broadview Editions series represents the ever-changing canon of literature by bringing together texts long regarded as classics with valuable lesser-known works.

Advisory editor for this volume: Denis Johnston

Broadview Press is an independent, international publishing house, incorporated in 1985. Broadview believes in shared ownership, both with its employees and with the general public; since the year 2000 Broadview shares have traded publicly on the Toronto Venture Exchange under the symbol BDP.

We welcome comments and suggestions regarding any aspect of our publications–please feel free to contact us at the addresses below or at broadview@broadviewpress.com / www.broadviewpress.com

North America
PO Box 1243, Peterborough, Ontario, Canada K9J 7H5
Tel: (705) 743-8990; Fax: (705) 743-8353
email: customerservice@broadviewpress.com
PO Box 1015, 3576 California Road, Orchard Park, NY, USA 14127

UK, Ireland, and continental Europe
NBN International
Estover Road
Plymouth PL6 7PY UK
Tel: 44 (0) 1752 202 300
Fax: 44 (0) 1752 202 330
email: enquiries@nbninternational.com

Australia and New Zealand
UNIREPS, University of New South Wales
Sydney, NSW, 2052
Australia
Tel: 61 2 9664 0999; Fax: 61 2 9664 5420
email: info.press@unsw.edu.au

Broadview Press gratefully acknowledges the financial support of the Government of Canada through the Book Publishing Industry Development Program for our publishing activities.

PRINTED IN CANADA

Contents

Acknowledgements

I would like to thank the Marblehead Museum and Historical Society, and especially its curator, Karen McInnis, for allowing me to examine the Bowen materials in that collection and to reproduce some of Ashley Bowen's watercolor paintings in this book. I am also deeply grateful to the Colonial Society of Massachusetts for allowing me to reproduce parts of their edition of *The Journals of Ashley Bowen (1728–1813) of Marblehead*, ed. Philip Chadwick Foster Smith, *Publications of the Colonial Society of Massachusetts*, vols. 44, 45 (Boston, 1973). Without the Society's public-spirited cooperation, this edition of Bowen's autobiography would never have been produced.

Foreword

It would be hard to identify an ordinary American working man of the colonial period who left behind a greater quantity and variety of written and illustrative material than Ashley Bowen of Marblehead, Massachusetts. Much of what he wrote and painted has been lost, but just the surviving items include sea journals and day-books, interleaved almanacs, miscellaneous reminiscences, letters, petitions, nearly a dozen watercolor paintings, and an illustrated autobiography. Together they cover an astounding 71 of the 85 years he spent on this earth and allow us to view an early American life almost from beginning to end in a depth that is seldom possible. On some important things, these surviving materials shed relatively faint light. Like most early American men he wrote little about the women in his life; his boyhood to the age of eleven remains a complete blank; and generally he preferred relating the course of events to revealing the state of his own feelings. Yet on paper he spoke of war, religion, politics, patriotism, community, marriage, disease, and especially, of course, his own history as a sailor and ship-rigger. One is unlikely to find a more detailed mirror of daily life in the lower ranks of colonial American society.

Amongst historians of New England, Ashley Bowen's writings are reasonably well-known. A quarter-century ago, Philip Chadwick Foster Smith published nearly all of them as *The Journals of Ashley Bowen* in the Colonial Society of Massachusetts' *Publications* series.[1] Most major university libraries own a copy of the edition, and a generation of scholars studying everything from seafaring to popular religion to manhood has drawn on this source.

Smith's publication of the *Journals* was a remarkable achievement. Over the years Bowen's papers had been scattered abroad and then collected by a half-dozen libraries and private individuals. Smith reassembled them and then reorganized everything before him in precise chronological order. He then set about transcribing the materials, following "neither a slavish adherence to the originals nor a

---

1 *The Journals of Ashley Bowen (1728–1813) of Marblehead*, ed. Philip Chadwick Foster Smith, *Publications of the Colonial Society of Massachusetts*, vols. 44, 45 (Boston, 1973).

complete modernization to current English-language usages."[1] Bowen had little formal schooling, hence his spelling was erratic and frequently phonetic (e.g., "scerss" for "scarce," "porseson" for "position," "Museles" for "Marseilles," and "Devrix" for "Devereaux"). To complicate matters, he often used abbreviations—some of which can today only be guessed at. The achievement of converting Bowen's difficult handwriting and Marblehead *patois* into readable, printed, modern English was Philip Smith's, not mine, and those who look through the pages of this Broadview edition are viewing one of the more remarkable editorial achievements in colonial American literature.

Although Smith summarized his editorial technique carefully in his own foreword, the reader of the Broadview edition needs to understand those of his basic principles carried over into this text.[2] First, spelling and capitalization have been corrected to modern usage, including proper names, except in the case of certain expressive terms used by Bowen and not found in any normal dictionary. Second, in cases where supplementary material is found in another Bowen source or in a distinct contemporary source such as a newspaper or a custom's house entry, that material is included in square brackets ([ ]). Third, grammar and syntax are preserved in their original forms, while questionable readings are followed by a question mark within square brackets, and illegible matter is represented as: ([...]). Fourth, in the case of shortened or misspelled words, where the meaning is clear they have been expanded or corrected to modern English.[3]

In addition, Smith traveled widely on both sides of the Atlantic, searching for supplementary and corroborative materials in newspapers, private papers, and a huge variety of public records relating to land, taxes, customs, pensions, public petitions, and naval activity, as well as births, marriages, and deaths, all of which he built into extensive footnotes and his own set of appendices. These materials focus principally on the events Bowen witnessed and the people he met. They are largely omitted from this volume, but they would certainly be of interest to anyone pursuing a particular topic in detail and can be found in the Colonial Society edition.

---

1 *Ibid.*, xv.

2 Smith's editorial technique is described in *ibid.*, v–xix.

3 For those interested, these rules are spelled out at some length with examples in *ibid.*, xv–xvii.

Why, the reader may ask, if Philip Smith did such a remarkable editorial job, do Ashley Bowen's writings merit a new and admittedly derivative publication? There are, in fact, several good reasons. The Smith edition is long—nearly 700 pages—and roughly two-thirds of it is composed of Bowen's fairly repetitive daily entries regarding mainly the operation of his ship-rigging loft in Marblehead. Though a model piece of scholarship, it is not really suited to casual reading or to classroom use. Furthermore, this Broadview edition presents the autobiography in its entirety, as a discrete whole, unlike the Smith edition, which melds it in with the rest of Bowen's writings. This is the real treasure amongst all of Ashley Bowen's papers, and the purpose of the Broadview edition is to present it in historical context. Part of that context is provided by the Introduction, which focuses on what we know about the maritime society of eighteenth-century America. The rest is furnished by the Appendices, which contain other materials from Bowen's diaries and miscellaneous papers as well as the writings of contemporaries who had encountered him or visited the town in which he lived. All of these sources help to situate the autobiography in time and to convey some of the breadth of its author's interests and experiences.

Bowen lived in an eventful age. He participated in several critical episodes in North American history—most notably the capture of Quebec in 1759—and he witnessed much else of interest during the decades that preceeded the American Revolution. Most importantly, he was the first common sailor in the British American colonies ever to write an autobiography detailed enough to open a window on that maritime world. There is no other source that manages this, and Ashley Bowen's self-portrait of a seafaring man's life in the eighteenth century deserves to be better known.

Introduction

Ashley Bowen was the first American mariner ever to recount the story of his life. At some point during the years following the American Revolution, probably when he was about sixty, having outlived two wives and most of his children, he sat down at his kitchen table surrounded by his journals and diaries and composed an autobiography of his life afloat and ashore. Beginning with his first voyage out of Boston as a ship's boy at the age of eleven, he recounted his personal experiences on land and sea over a span of more than thirty years, illustrated with watercolors painted from memory of every vessel on which he had ever sailed.

In many ways, Bowen was a very ordinary fellow: his experience on the deep mirrored that of hundreds of other young men who grew up along the Massachusetts coastline in the eighteenth century. He went to sea as a boy, fished, whaled, worked in both the merchant and the naval service, took up a landward trade after he quit the sea, helped to raise a family, and died no more than a few minutes' walk from where he was born. Where he differed from the rest of his mates was in his fondness for writing and his decision to save his journals and papers for posterity. Before his death, he seems to have handed these writings over to his friend, the Rev. William Bentley of Salem, and, through channels unclear, a great many of them have survived to the present. They include ships' journals, daily diaries, poetry, letters, drawings, and vivid accounts of his dreams, as well as the autobiography. Together, they leave us a remarkable view of one mariner's life in detail—remarkable not because Ashley Bowen accomplished memorable deeds, but because he memorialized so many of his ordinary deeds, the sort that any common sailor of his day might have encountered. These may seem extraordinary enough by our sedentary modern standards, but they would have fallen well within the realm of the expected in his day.

Ashley Bowen's autobiography differs from the stories of seafaring with which we are most familiar principally because it accepts the sea as a given. Like most people who grew up in maritime communities during the age of sail, Bowen did not feel any need to explain or justify his decision to go to sea: it was simply what he had done. The picture we possess of the mariner's lot was largely painted in the nineteenth century by authors such as James Fenimore Cooper, Richard Henry Dana, Jr., and Herman Melville, all of whom grew up in an America that was becoming a profoundly continental country for which the sea was mainly a boundary. To go to sea in their day was an exceptional choice—occasioned with growing frequency by special circumstances and individual disposition. Men poor in property, boys intent on proving their manhood, youths afflicted with wanderlust, and ethnic outsiders facing discrimination on shore came to constitute the majority of crews on board American vessels, and together these men seemed, in the increasingly continental culture of the United States, to be a breed apart. To Ashley Bowen, by contrast, sailors and fishermen were not a "strange race of men": they were his neighbors, who went to sea, as did many young men in coastal communities throughout the early modern world, because in such an environment it seemed the most logical apprenticeship for adult life.[1] Hence, the autobiography does not begin with any apology: it simply describes without fanfare how he obtained his first berth. The story of his seafaring career, though full of incident, is recounted without romantic overtones, and there is in the entire text none of the ethnography of mariners that became such a prominent feature of the seafaring genre in the nineteenth century. Bowen had a lively mind, and he recounted many remarkable stories, but he never felt the need to explain the sailor's lot: in the society in which he grew up, most people understood it already.

Ashley Bowen's autobiography also differs from the more familiar narratives of maritime life in that it is not much of a travelogue. Most mariners' memoirs of any period have always devoted considerable space to the places they visited and the people they met. Prior to the invention of modern media, ordinary folk learned much of what they knew about the wider world, either directly from the stories sailors told about their voyages, or indirectly from the memoirs that found publishers and readers. Although Bowen traveled widely

---

1 Quotation from *Wood et al. v. the Nimrod* (1829), *Federal Cases, Comprising Cases Argued and Determined in the Circuit and District Courts of the United States ...*, 30 vols., 30: 471. For a thoughtful analysis of why nineteenth-century Americans went to sea, see Margaret Creighton, *Rites and Passages: The Experience of American Whaling, 1830–1870* (Cambridge: Cambridge UP, 1995).

around the North Atlantic basin and encountered a variety of different cultures in Western Europe, the Caribbean islands, the Mediterranean region, and the mainland colonies of North America from Canada to the Carolinas, he spilled little ink describing them for his audience. Perhaps he was just inattentive, but more probably he was writing about places and peoples with whom his local audience would already have been quite familiar, since so many had sailed in the same trades as he. Ashley Bowen's life was full of dramatic incident, but he never regarded his path through it as unusual, and like most seafaring men of the eighteenth century he took the variety of human experience for granted.

★ ★ ★

At the end of the colonial period, Marblehead, Massachusetts, was the largest commercial fishing port in North America. In February or March of every year, 1,200 men in 150 schooners set sail from its comfortable harbor, and over the ensuing nine months until winter closed in again they fished for cod on the great offshore banks of the Northwest Atlantic. All the fish they landed—probably somewhere in the order of 25,000 metric tonnes annually—they carried back to Marblehead to be dried in large commercial fishyards scattered through the town. When the cod had been cured and packed in huge barrels called hogsheads, another fleet of trading vessels—larger schooners and brigantines, also locally owned and crewed—shipped the fish abroad, some to the West Indies and even more to Spain. Taken together, these fishing schooners and merchant craft, together with the fishyards, shipyards, and rigging lofts where the vessels were maintained, employed most men of working age in the town.[1]

Marblehead was a tough community. This may be hard to imagine, given the upscale yachting-centered flavor of the place today, but almost every traveler who passed through it in Bowen's time remarked on three features: its rugged and irregular layout, the poverty of its inhabitants, and the swarms of children underfoot.

1 On the history of Marblehead, see Christine Leigh Heyrman, *Commerce and Culture: The Maritime Communities of Colonial Massachusetts, 1690–1750* (New York: Norton, 1984); Daniel Vickers, *Farmers and Fishermen: Two Centuries of Work in Essex County, Massachusetts, 1630–1850* (Chapel Hill, NC: U of North Carolina P 1994).

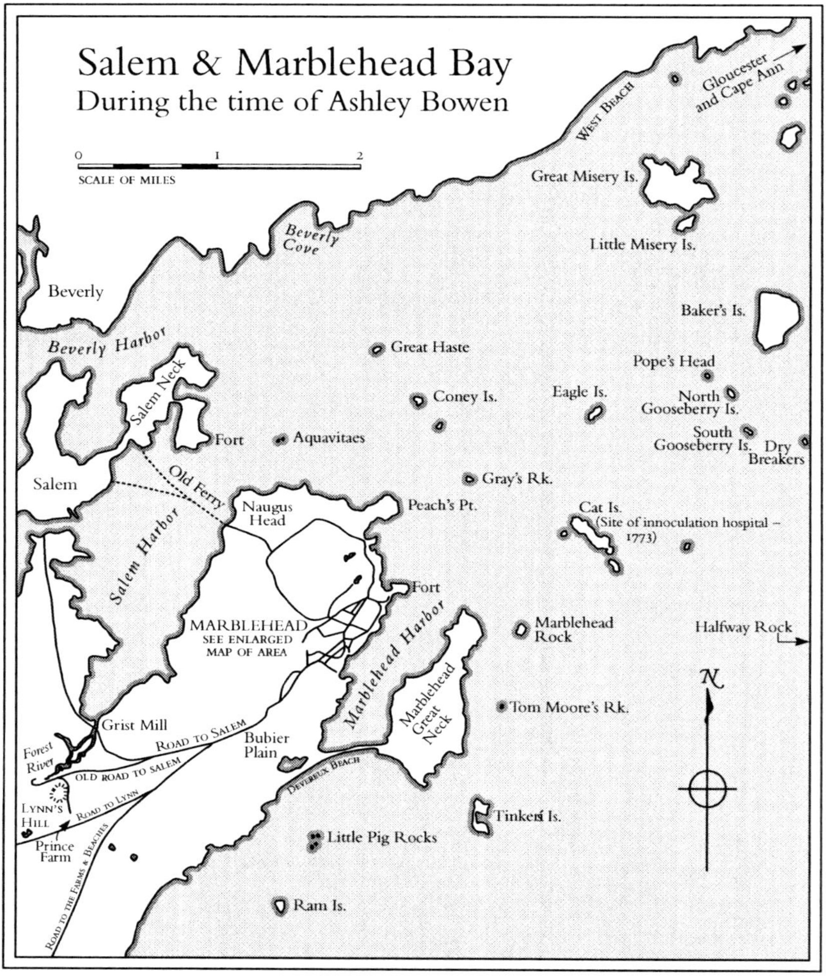

Founded by fishermen on a rough and stony peninsula, chosen more for its harbor and its proximity to good fishing than for good soil and gentle terrain, the town was composed mainly of small and shabby clapboard houses, tucked in among the rocks and connected by a maze of crooked streets. Through most of the year, the air was filled with the smell of cod drying on rough tables in the fishyards about town. Here and there a wealthy merchant might construct a grander home—the Jeremiah Lee mansion was one of the most sumptuous ever constructed in colonial New England—but most of Lee's neighbors lived in very different circumstances. The majority of Marblehead mariners and fishermen dwelt with their families in rented rooms, plainly furnished with the basic necessities of life and little else. Few owned more than two or three changes of clothing, and nearly all were confined to a repetitive diet of salt meat and fish, bread and root vegetables eaten off earthenware plates. Entertainment consisted mainly of neighborly cordiality lubricated with rum.

Ashley Bowen was born in 1728 into what was by local standards a privileged family. His father Nathan had served an apprenticeship in a Boston counting house and then for reasons unknown had moved ten miles north along the coast in 1718 to settle in Marblehead. There he purchased a home several blocks back from the waterfront, to which in 1719 he brought his young wife, a Boston merchant's daughter named Sarah Ashley. In Marblehead Nathan built a career as a trader, gentleman, notary public, justice of the peace, teacher of navigation, and author of almanacs. At some point he acquired a farm of more than 100 acres near the south end of town along the road to Boston, and so could be termed a gentleman farmer as well. In the opinion of one of his daughters, Nathan Bowen was "too much taken up with the things of this world," (Appendix G1) and the relationship between him and his son Ashley seems never to have been very warm. The one letter from the elder Bowen that survives from the correspondence they exchanged in later years (Appendix G2) displays a perfunctory tone, and the infrequency with which Ashley mentioned his father in his daily journal suggests that as adults they never spent much time together. Nathan's final decline and death in 1776 were noted briefly with "my honored father quite low in health" one day, "quite ill" the next, and "departed this life, aged seventy-eight years and eight months and eight days" the day after that. Ashley was never given to emotional outbursts on paper, but from the day of the funeral (at which Nathan was borne to the grave by some of the richest men in town) through the remainder of his writings, he hardly ever mentioned his father again.[1]

---

1 Philip Chadwick Foster Smith, ed., *The Journals of Ashley Bowen (1728–1813) of Marblehead*, 2 vols. (Colonial Society of Massachusetts, *Publications*, 44–45 [Boston: Colonial Society of Massachusetts 1973]), 45: 506.

Ashley Bowen's feelings about his childhood remain invisible. We know that he had two older brothers and five mostly younger sisters, and we also know that his mother, Sarah, died in childbirth when he was only twelve. The manner in which he described this tragedy as "the greatest part of my ruining" (Autobiography, p. 37) may imply that their relationship was close. Ashley's younger sister Elizabeth remembered their mother as "a meek & humble christian" and a "tender guide" (Appendix G1). In the contrast between that image and Ashley's characterization of his *step*mother (whom Nathan married shortly after Sarah's death) as a "fine, rich widow," (Autobiography, p. 37), we may perhaps sense something of what, with his own mother's passing, Ashley had lost. But because the memoir opens abruptly in 1739, just after his eleventh birthday, we can only guess at how his boyhood was actually experienced. Really only one aspect of Ashley's childhood is indisputable—the fact that he grew up beside the sea.

Yet this point matters, because during the age of sail the widely shared trait of seaside origins was what channeled most sailors into the seafaring life. As little boys, they encountered the ocean by swimming from the shore, fishing from the rocks, or punting about in boats. Their fathers did much of the regular business of the household—fetching wood, hauling provisions, freighting hay, shopping, or simply visiting friends—in small craft, rowing or sailing down rivers, across harbors, or along the coast; and as the boys grew older, they learned to lend a hand upon the water. At some point in their teenage years, the majority of them tried their luck on the deep, perhaps signing on for a trip of a few weeks along the coast, a fishing expedition of several months, or even a voyage overseas that could occupy the better part of a year. Some found that a single stint at sea was enough, but others persisted, for any number of reasons—the chance to build a career, the lack of other opportunities ashore, the love of adventure, or just a simple curiosity about foreign parts. It would be wrong, however, to associate the decision to go to sea in Bowen's day with any special compulsion—material or spiritual—or to assume that seamen were necessarily indigent and deracinated. Almost all of them had grown up in households where physical work was part of life, but as many were from modestly propertied artisanal or farming families as came from the ranks of the laboring poor. Going to sea would have been as normal in a town like Marblehead as a craft apprenticeship or a term of farm service would have been in a rural village inland.[1]

Ashley was luckier than some in that his father could afford to place him as an apprentice to a Boston shipmaster, who was to teach him the art and mystery of navigation. But as readers will discover, Capt. Peter Hall was a less than ideal choice, and Ashley's years in his service were neither instructive nor happy. Hall was interested in the boy only as a personal servant and taught him next to nothing about the business of commerce or the practice of running a ship. Moreover, the captain had an ugly temper and beat Ashley over trivial matters—severely enough that the incidents stuck in the latter's memory for decades. The mere fact of physical punishment would not have struck a colonial youth as unusual: what the law termed "moderate chastisement" was a master's prerogative on land and sea in the Atlantic world of the period. Labor discipline throughout New England retained, well into the nineteenth century, the patriarchal character of being personal, physical, and arbitrary. What bothered Ashley was the unjust imbalance between the minor nature of his offenses—burning a dinner or dirtying some towels—and the lashings someone little more than a boy received for them. How common such events were at sea is difficult to judge, but it is interesting to note that these boyhood beatings at the hands of Capt. Hall were the only ones Bowen remembered, at least well enough to record, in all his years under sail.[2]

Ashley Bowen's maritime career, which was launched when he turned eleven and concluded when he reached the age of thirty-five, was marked by astonishing variety. At different times he worked as a fisherman, whaleman, boatman, coaster, deep-water mariner, and midshipman in the British navy. He traveled to dozens of different seaports around the Atlantic and the Mediterranean, and he spent considerable time ashore in a number of different spots as a storekeeper, house plasterer, student of navigation, and even prisoner. Yet, although he saw much of the world, he never achieved what he

---

1 On the background of eighteenth-century Massachusetts seafarers, see Daniel Vickers, *Young Men and the Sea: Yankee Seafarers in the Age of Sail* (New Haven, CT: Yale UP, 2005): 96–162.

2 *Ibid.*, 220–26.

wanted most—to become a shipmaster himself. In New England seaports such as Marblehead, the proportion of seamen who managed to climb to the quarterdeck during the colonial period was surprisingly high. Many careers were cut short by shipwreck, accident, or disease, but amongst those mariners who stuck to the sea and avoided disaster, the odds of rising some day to captain a vessel were better than even. Yet, in spite of his well-to-do father, his persistence at sea, and his own good health, Ashley never really made it. Once in 1756 he commanded a West Indian sloop on a voyage home to Marblehead, and a couple of times during the Seven Years War he served as master of a coaster transporting men and goods to and from Quebec. With these exceptions, however, he worked out his seafaring career in a supporting role, either as seaman or mate, and when he quit the sea at the age of thirty-five, he had little to show for his pains. It was only through commanding a vessel that most mariners were ever able to take part in the commerce they managed and to prosper from their voyages. Although most shipmasters never grew wealthy, they could usually obtain enough credit to purchase hogsheads of fish, bales of cloth, or barrels of molasses to carry along and sell in distant ports, and over the years they might well manage to settle their families at home in reasonably comfortable circumstances. For common seamen and lesser officers, however, that sort of status—what New Englanders liked to call a competency—was difficult to achieve. Seen in that light, it makes sense for Bowen to have decided in 1763 to give up voyaging and try his luck ashore.[1]

During the age of sail, work afloat demanded a wider range of talents then we often imagine. Full-rigged ships carried specialist craftsmen, but on the smaller vessels of the sort that Bowen shipped on everything necessary to sustain life at sea had to be handled by the crew alone. Hence, seamen learned not only to hand, reef, and steer, but also the range of skills necessary to keep a vessel in repair. Any mariner with a dozen years under his belt would have become a not-so-amateur carpenter, sailmaker, rigger, cooper, boatbuilder, and shipwright. Practicing such a trade on shore successfully would

1 Daniel Vickers and Vince Walsh, "Young Men and the Sea: The Sociology of Seafaring in Eighteenth-Century Salem, Massachusetts," *Social History*, 24 (1999): 17–38. For a graphic representation of Bowen's seafaring years that demonstrates how much time he spent ashore, see Vickers, *Young Men and the Sea*, 100–03.

require connections and some capital, which not every retired sailor possessed; but in a smaller port like Marblehead, it was possible in rented quarters with borrowed money to launch a second career of some sort, and this was clearly what Ashley had in mind.

One important thing that had happened to Ashley in 1758 both hastened and made possible his decision to settle on shore: he got married. Although the details of his rather remarkable courtship of Dorothy Chadwick can be followed in the text (Appendix A), it is important to understand the wider significance of marriage in a New England mariner's life. Although seafarers may have had a reputation for being footloose and unattached, much of this stemmed less from any cultural proclivity for masculine liberty than it did from the simple truth that the majority of sailors were young men who had not yet settled down. Amongst crews from neighboring Salem, the median age of seamen in Bowen's day was only 22. Some of these young men would lose their lives, either to accident or to disease, and never start a family, but for the remainder marriage was the norm, at a median age of 24. Indeed, by waiting until the year he turned thirty, Bowen was decidedly slow in choosing a spouse. But marriage did not simply attract men home to shore: it could also make that decision easier. Launching oneself in certain waterfront trades could be difficult to manage without a wife. Any mariner who opened a shop, ran a tavern, or took in boarders without a partner skilled in domestic arts or willing and able to run the place during his absence would be operating at serious disadvantage. In maritime New England, moreover, credit was easier for a man to obtain once he was wed. Marriage implied not only roots in the community but also the likely existence of property—either a home or at least the furnishings of a household—that could be seized if the debtor defaulted. Mariners who hoped to manage ashore would find it a lot easier if storekeepers, merchants, and landlords would trust them with credit, and this was something that a family would facilitate.[1]

With a household to support and a wife to assist him, in the 1760s Ashley embarked on a second career ashore as a ship rigger. Having learned about repairing the lines and ropes he had labored with on dozens of vessels during his quarter-century afloat, he now set about

1 Vickers, *Young Men and the Sea*, 116, 266.

fashioning whole suits of rigging for other vessels in a rented loft in Marblehead. Taking orders from different shipowners—whose acquaintance he had made during his career at sea—he would lay out the cordage with the appropriate wooden blocks and assemble them together into shrouds, stays, halyards, sheets, and the many other lines that a full-rigged vessel required. The other half of the business, conducted largely by his wife Dorothy, was the manufacture of flags and pendants—what Ashley called "colors"—for the same market. The last decade before the American Revolution was boom time in Marblehead and prosperous for the Bowens. Save for the dead of winter when most vessels were idle and work in an unheated loft was next to impossible, they were busy almost all the time—often so much so Ashley had to hire additional help.

Bowen was probably more successful than most retired sailors at launching a second career ashore. The shreds of evidence on the subsequent careers of his contemporaries suggest that most of them never practiced any trade on land long enough ever to be formally identified with rigging, sailmaking, shoemaking, or any other shoreside trade. The more successful mariners in New England—those who rose to command vessels of their own and were able to accumulate some capital—settled into small businesses as shopkeepers on the waterfront or shoremen with fishyards for drying and curing cod. But the majority—either too poor in property or physically worn down by their years at sea—never found anything more than casual employment on shore, and once their seafaring days were over depended chiefly on their children for maintenance. Following a series of terrible winter storms in the late 1760s, the town of Marblehead petitioned the Massachusetts government for a tax abatement precisely because of the "many Parents deprived of the earnings of their Sons, which was their chief support." Retired seafarers in Ashley Bowen's New England returned to their families: they were not mainly wanderers, wastrels or drunkards consigned to the gutter. But like most working people of the eighteenth century, they found life an uphill struggle on a slope that grew steeper and rougher as they aged.[1]

In one respect, Bowen was unusually lucky in that he managed to age at all. Mortality was high everywhere in the early modern world

---

1 *Essex Gazette*, 19–26 June 1770.

but particularly so amongst young men in seaport towns. Detailed parish records from neighboring Salem during the eighteenth century suggest that any young seaman who had survived to the age of twenty stood a 30 per cent chance of dying within the next ten years. Although some of these deaths resulted from accident or combat—the sort we associate with storms, shipwrecks, pirates, and privateers—the deadliest enemy of any early modern mariner who ventured into the tropics was disease. On the Caribbean voyages that at one time or another almost every New England sailor traveled, yellow fever and malaria carried by mosquitoes were the principal killers. Indeed, the closest Bowen ever came to death was inside the French colonial prison in St. Domingue where he was several times thought to have been carried off by the "fever and ague." Not every landfall was equally dangerous. Those who sailed in more temperate regions—the Baltic Sea or the New England coast itself—ran fewer risks, but other stretches of the Atlantic rim were even deadlier than the Caribbean. Of West Africa it was said one should:

> Beware and take care
> Of the Bight of Benin;
> For one that goes out,
> There are forty go in.[1]

Although neither Bowen nor any other sailor-journalist ever dwelt on their fears of dying, it is hard to imagine that the plain demographic reality of their trade escaped them. Possessed by what Richard Henry Dana, Jr. once termed "overstrained manliness," they may have avoided talking about it much in public, but the prospect of dying young must have preyed on their minds. Ashley was fortunate: he carried on to the age of 85. But in doing so he outlived *six* of his eight sons. How fatherhood could have been borne in such conditions stretches the modern imagination.[2]

There were several other peculiar elements of maritime society—beyond the basic tragedy of early death—that hung on such elevated

1 Cited in Marcus Rediker, *Between the Devil and the Deep Blue Sea: Merchant Seamen, Pirates, and the Anglo-American Maritime World, 1700–1750* (Cambridge: Cambridge UP, 1987), 47.

2 Richard Henry Dana, Jr., *Two Years Before the Mast* (Harmondsworth: Penguin, 1981), 330.

mortality. One, oddly enough, was opportunity. It was the disappearance of so many foremast hands that reduced the competition for officers' posts and enhanced for the lucky survivors the chances of promotion. A second was the burden that mortality placed on the families and communities affected. Everywhere in early modern times, the deaths of young people compounded the normal difficulties of household survival by ensuring that only a reduced number of hungry children ever grew up to become productive adults. This was surely the dilemma faced by the old woman in the shoe, "who had so many children she didn't know what to do." In seaports like Marblehead, the mortality of young mariners forced most of their brothers to forgo formal apprenticeships and sign on to fishing or merchant voyages where they could earn enough money to enable parents—frequently widowed or disabled—to sustain their families. The dangers of the seafaring life generated therefore both the incentive of promotion that drew men to sea and the chronic shortage of household income that gave them no other choice.

⋆ ⋆ ⋆

Bowen's life spanned some of the most eventful years in the history of the Thirteen Colonies and the new United States. The episode he actually participated in and plainly believed to be the climax of his active seafaring career was the British conquest of Canada during the Seven Years War. He enlisted in the expedition against Quebec in the summer of 1759, witnessed the Battle of the Plains of Abraham on September 13, and saw the French surrender the city several days later. Although Bowen could not have realized it at the time, he had witnessed the central event in the establishment of British hegemony over most of North America and (through the removal of the French threat and the need for British protection) a key stage in the movement towards American independence. Moreover, although his own role in events was of a supporting nature, he played it in the company of one of the great figures of his time—the famous Pacific explorer, Captain James Cook. During the Canada expedition, Cook was placed in charge of surveying the St. Lawrence River aboard the *H.M.S. Pembroke*, on which Bowen was midshipman. To the end of his life Ashley boasted of the service he had performed under the direction of one of the most celebrated individuals the eighteenth century produced.

The other world-historical event Bowen witnessed was, of course, the American Revolution. During the final years of the colonial period, running from 1766 to the outbreak of the War of Independence and through to 1778, Ashley Bowen kept an uninterrupted diary devoted to the comings and goings in Marblehead harbor, the daily rhythms of work inside his loft, and the news of importance he heard about town. This journal is lengthy and repetitive: consequently only small parts of it are included in this volume. Still, Bowen's choice over what to include and exclude in his treatment of events illuminates the coming of the Revolution in New England in a way that stands somewhat apart from conventional treatments of the subject, and it deserves our attention.

In the first place, one has to be struck by Bowen's near total silence regarding the American resistance. We are accustomed to dealing with the years between the close of the Seven Years War and the opening of the War of Independence as almost entirely framed by imperial politics and colonial response. That is how textbooks treat the period; it is also the focus of scholarly discussion. Yet Bowen's diary, in spite of having been composed in a town just a few hours by water from Boston, where so many of the critical events leading to revolution occurred, makes almost no reference to any acts of resistance before the spring of 1774. None of the larger parliamentary milestones in the march to revolution (the Sugar Act of 1764, the Stamp Act of 1765, the Declaratory Act of 1766, the Townshend Act of 1767, or the Tea Act of 1773) nor any of the prominent incidents of popular resistance (the Stamp Act Riots of 1765, the Boston Massacre of 1770, or the Boston Tea Party of 1773) moved Bowen sufficiently to prompt an entry from his pen. In 1769 an incident aboard a Marblehead vessel, in which a naval officer attempting to impress four Irish-born residents of the town was killed by a harpoon through the neck, resulted in one of the more celebrated trials of the revolutionary period. When the mariners were brought to trial and defended by John Adams, they were acquitted by a local jury on the grounds of justifiable homicide. Yet neither when the event occurred in April, nor when the trial was held in June, did Bowen ever make mention of the event. With the benefit of hindsight we today may understand the significance of the resistance narrative, but obviously Bowen did not. Until the passage of the Coercive Acts in 1774, he did not suspect that anything critical was afoot.[1]

The single biggest news item in Marblehead during these years, which had nothing directly to do with imperial politics, was the smallpox epidemic of 1773 and the controversy surrounding the founding of an inoculation hospital. Bowen devoted far more space in his diary to this controversy than to any other event in the final decade of the colonial period, and as it mattered to him, it deserves some exploration here. The smallpox epidemic itself broke out during the summer of 1773, coincidentally, in the home of Ashley Bowen's mother-in-law. The pox was a terrible disease—highly contagious, extraordinarily painful, hideous to the sight, fatal to perhaps one-fifth of all those afflicted, and permanently disfiguring to those who survived. In August, the rising death toll prompted four wealthy residents of town—John and Jonathan Glover, Elbridge Gerry, and Azor Orne—to form a partnership and build a hospital on Cat Island about a half-mile off the tip of Marblehead Neck for the purpose of inoculating healthy townspeople against the threat of infection. Inoculation works by implanting the live smallpox virus directly under the skin, which for reasons still incompletely understood produces a milder and usually survivable form of the disease followed by lifetime immunity. This was a riskier procedure than vaccination, the method of using cowpox virus to produce the same immunity (later introduced by Edward Jenner in 1798), but it usually worked if administered in a controlled and isolated environment. The Essex Hospital (or Castle Pox, as Ashley Bowen termed it) was completed in early October, and the proprietors hired Dr. Hall Jackson, an English-trained physician from Portsmouth, New Hampshire, to supervise the procedure.[2]

Even before the hospital was opened, however, some townspeople began to voice their opposition. Some were worried by the

---

1 Christopher P. Magra, "'Soldiers ... Bred to the Sea': Maritime Marblehead, Massachusetts, and the Origins and Progress of the American Revolution," *New England Quarterly*, 77 (2004): 531–34, 542–44; Smith, ed., *Journals of Ashley Bowen*, 44: 208–14.

2 On smallpox in the eighteenth century, see Elizabeth A. Fenn, *Pox Americana: The Great Smallpox Epidemic of 1775–1782* (New York: Hill and Wang, 2001); George A. Billias, Pox and Politics in Marblehead," *Essex Institute Historical Collections* 92 (1956): 45–46.

danger of actually spreading the disease (if infection escaped the controlled environment of the hospital); others claimed that the cost of inoculation (about a year's income for a fisherman to have his family treated) meant that only the rich would benefit; and still others suspected that the proprietors only aimed at lining their own pockets at the townspeople's expense. Recriminations between the supporters and enemies of the hospital flew back and forth throughout the fall, but the struggle rapidly came to a head in January 1774 when four men were caught stealing infected bedding from the island. The guilty were tarred and feathered and paraded through the streets, and then about a week later a mob attacked the hospital itself and burnt it to the ground. When the proprietors served a writ on two of the arsonists and had them incarcerated in Salem, an armed crowd of several hundred people marched there from Marblehead, assaulted the jail, freed the men, and agreed to lay down their weapons only when the proprietors dropped all charges relating to the case.[1]

Bowen was so taken up with epidemic and riot between June 1773 and March 1774 that he never once mentioned the train of events that ran from the passage of the Tea Act in London to the Boston Tea Party. If he knew what was going on in the provincial capital and the wider world, he never thought it worthy of record. With the news of the Coercive Acts, however, the imperial conflict moved to center stage both in the town of Marblehead and in Ashley Bowen's mind. Unlike every previous act of Parliament, these four pieces of legislation had a direct and serious impact on the day-to-day conduct of government and matters of everyday life within the colony. Together, they made the provincial council appointive, restricted town meetings to one a year, allowed for the billeting of troops in private homes, permitted British officials to be tried outside the colony, and closed the port of Boston to all trade except for foodstuffs. General Thomas Gage arrived in May 1774 to take over the governorship of Massachusetts, and from that point forward, Bowen's diary reported on political events regularly. Within Marblehead the most dramatic new development was the conversion of the town into an official port of entry and the arrival of the

1 Billias, "Pox and Politics," 47–54.

customs officers and troops needed to enforce the law. As the year wore on, Bowen began to record with steady frequency the protests of townspeople up and down the coast, the arrival of troops by sea, and the ominous movements of British naval vessels offshore. In April of 1775, after the battles of Lexington and Concord, the British began to blockade Marblehead harbor in earnest and to impress local inhabitants into the naval service. Finally in July, the Restraining Act shut the fisheries down completely, commerce ground to a halt, and most Marblehead men of fighting age—by now thoroughly disenchanted with British policy—marched off to join the Continental Army or signed on with privateers.

From the day General Gage landed in Boston, Bowen was alarmed by everything he saw. Crowds of British regulars marching through the town, press gangs seizing his neighbors off the wharfs, vessels exchanging cannon-fire off the coast—these were in his words "terrible times." And for the most part he blamed the patriots for the conflict. In his opinion the leaders of the American resistance were self-interested poseurs, a "stern foremost gentry" playing at war with an opponent they could not really hope to defeat. Ashley's experience in the Seven Years War had convinced him that the British military and naval forces were unbeatable and that his countrymen would only suffer by taking them on. Indeed, from the outbreak of hostilities he almost always reported news from the front in a negative light—that is, as British victories and American defeats. Early in 1775, for example, a party of redcoats led by one Col. Leslie was turned back at Salem's North Bridge by a crowd of angry patriots in an event known as "Leslie's Retreat." Bowen heard of the story and took note of it, but in his rendition, the British marched up to the bridge, crossed it, "marched over as far as they pleased and returned back again." The Battle of Bunker Hill the following year he described, not as a patriot triumph, but rather as the burning of Charlestown followed by an American retreat. When the British actually abandoned Massachusetts in March 1776, Bowen described the event impressively as the departure of "55 sail of shipping from below Boston," without ever remarking that New England was now effectively independent. In his view, challenging Britain was wrong in large part because it could never succeed.

The other issue that colored Bowen's response to the revolutionary movement and the War of Independence was religion. Bowen's father was a Baptist and as a consequence Ashley was never baptized as a child (Appendix G1). His older sister, Molly, attempted to have him baptized as a New Light Congregationalist when he was a teenager during the Great Awakening, but Capt. Peter Hall, an Anglican and Ashley's master at the time, forbade it. Instead, on Christmas Eve, 1744, during a period when Bowen was helping keep store in Port Mahon on Minorca, Hall arranged to have his apprentice christened within the Church of England. Ashley made no further mention of religion in the autobiography, not did he record in his diaries attending church on a regular basis until his early forties. Churchgoing was next to impossible for a sailor on the move, and the limited role that formal religion played in his youth probably distinguished him little from most of his Marblehead neighbors. In 1771, the year that his first wife Dorothy died, Sunday entries began to appear in his diary, and from his early forties onward—as a waterfront artisan with a growing family—the quality of his faith seems to have deepened.

When the War of Independence broke out, the matter of Anglican observance became a political issue, because as a church it was headed by George III, now king of an enemy power. Patriots on the whole were willing to tolerate Sunday services within this denomination as long as ministers dropped all solicitations for the king and royal family contained in the Book of Common Prayer. Unfortunately for Bowen, the Anglican minister in Marblehead, William Weeks, took a hard line on this matter, refused to drop the prayers in question, and eventually patriots forced St. Michael's, the local Anglican church, to close its doors. Bowen was deeply angered by what he plainly considered an attack on his religious liberties, and he was so worried that his own creed would be eradicated from the land that he actually set out to copy by hand the entire Book of Common Prayer. In 1776 when justifying his reticence about adopting the patriot cause, he explained his position almost entirely in terms of his faith (Appendix E2). His religious beliefs and the political views he drew from them cost him dearly during the war—in the straining of personal relations around town and even perhaps in the collapse of his rigging business. We are not accustomed to thinking of sailors as caring much about religion, but Bowen plainly did, and he may not have been alone.[1]

But was Bowen a loyalist? To judge by his reflections of later years, he certainly seems closer to the Tory than to the Patriot end of the spectrum (Appendix G4). During the Revolutionary War, however, he judged the American cause mainly in terms of its impact on Marblehead. Even in his language, he employed "we" to represent, not loyalists or patriots, but the people of his home town regardless of whether they were pursuing British shipping on the high seas or fraternizing with the King's troops on shore. Throughout the war, Bowen managed to maintain friendships on both sides of the political divide, and although he plainly believed he would have been happier under the empire, there is no evidence he ever felt that independence would compel him to leave. Between the British Navy and the Continental Army, the parochial world that mattered most to him was caught in the middle. In a personal turn of phrase he lamented in August of 1775: "Only between two stools our ass comes to the grounds. Poor, poor, oh poor Marblehead!" (Appendix D3)

From Bowen's perspective, the years of the Revolutionary War did, indeed, prove calamitous. Marblehead was devastated by the conflict. By 1780, half of the 831 men in town were unemployed, a further 166 lay in British prisons, and 121 were missing; of the 1,069 female residents a staggering 378 were widows; and out of 2,242 children, a total of 672 were fatherless.[2] When peace arrived in 1783, Bowen's ship-rigging business lay in tatters, and it was never effectively rebuilt. In personal terms, Ashley was now estranged from many of his neighbors; his eldest son had vanished—probably killed at sea; and his second wife had died from causes unknown. Even his church had barely survived. The entries in his diary shortened noticeably, and after 2 January 1796 they ceased altogether, though perhaps the later volumes have simply been lost. Bowen never recovered the prosperity he had enjoyed before the war, and by 1804 he was, in his own words, now living "under bare poles," almost certainly dependent on his children for support. The old mariner

1 For differing opinions on the importance of religion to early modern mariners, see Alain Cabantous, *Le ciel dans la mer: Christianisme et civilisation maritime, XVIe-XIXe siècle* (Paris: Fayard, 1990); and Rediker, *Between the Devil and the Deep Blue Sea*, 169–86.

2 Smith, ed., *Journals of Ashley Bowen*, 45: 551.

died at the age of 85 on 2 February 1813. Remaining to the end a man of unfixed views, he asked that the Congregationalist parson pray at his house and the Episcopalian minister preside at the grave. He chose to be buried in the grounds of the Congregationalist New Meeting House so as to be close to his kindred, but the stone itself was set to face St. Michael's Church.[1]

Ashley Bowen was not a typical mariner: such a person does not exist. Still, his life should remind us of some truths that conventional wisdom on seafaring history may have overlooked. The first is that most sailors spent most of their lives ashore. Even a career mariner like Bowen, who went to sea at eleven and retired from it at thirty-five, spent all of his childhood, significant stretches of his youth and young manhood, and most of his later years on land. The peculiar environment of the ship created an occupational culture that shaped Bowen profoundly, but it was not the only cultural force that bore on his life. It does not explain his attachment to the Church of England, his deep parochialism, his opposition to medical innovation, his suspicion of republicanism, or the significance of family. The decision to go to sea is usually construed as a break from the past—from the often stifling ties of parish, community, and kin—but Bowen's quarter-century of seafaring snapped none of those.

Maybe he was just an odd fish. Yet, perhaps he just seems that way because, under the influence of the romantic portrait drawn by the great sea-authors of the nineteenth century, we have come to associate "maritime" too exclusively with the sea itself. We hang more on the socializing power of the ship, in other words, than it can possibly bear. The word "maritime," however, has an alternative meaning in relation to people, which is "living near or by the sea," and during the age of sail this second definition captures not only the relatively homogeneous nature of the sea-going experience, but also the remarkably heterogeneous character of life ashore.[2] It encourages us, not to generalize about a single maritime culture, but to imagine how the great variety of maritime societies—around New England, around the Atlantic, and around the world—were

1 William Bentley, *The Diary of William Bentley, D.D.: Pastor of the East Church, Salem, Massachusetts,* 4 vols. (Salem, 1905–14; rpt. Gloucester, MA: P. Smith, 1962), 3: 125; 4: 148–49.

2 *OED Online* (2nd ed., 2005).

interconnected yet different. Ashley Bowen was not primarily a man *of* the sea: he lived *beside* the sea, amongst a particular group of neighbors and kin in a particular community that pursued a particular set of trades. Even the course of his years afloat was shaped by the environment from which his voyaging was launched. On the deepest level that was what "maritime" meant to most ordinary seafaring men in the age of sail.

Ashley Bowen: A Brief Chronology

1728	Ashley Bowen born
1739	Ashley Bowen's first voyage
1739–48	King George's War
1754–63	Seven Years War
1758	Ashley Bowen marries Dorothy Chadwick
1759	Ashley and Dorothy Bowen's first child born
1759	Fall of Quebec
1763	Ashley Bowen quits the sea to become a ship-rigger in Marblehead
1765	Stamp Act Riots
1771	Dorothy Bowen dies; Ashley marries Mary Shaw
1773	Boston Tea Party
1773–74	Smallpox epidemic in Marblehead
1774	Coercive Acts
1775	Battles of Lexington, Concord, and Bunker Hill
1775–83	American War of Independence
1776	Declaration of Independence
1781	Mary Bowen dies
1782	Ashley Bowen marries Hannah Graves
1787	United States Constitutional Convention in Philadelphia
1789	Outbreak of the French Revolution
1792–1815	French Revolutionary and Napoleonic Wars
1797	Ashley and Hannah Bowen's final child born
1813	Ashley Bowen dies

THE AUTOBIOGRAPHY OF ASHLEY BOWEN

(1728–1813)

1728

According to my father's statement of matters, I was born on the 8 of January this year in a house that he and one Cogswell built that the late Thomas Bartlett, painter, owned not far from the brick ponds in Marblehead the first year of King George the Second.

1739

In March the snow[1] *Marblehead*, Captain Staly, was cast away on Ipswich beach, the captain lost, &c. This summer, as my father taught the art of navigation, Captain Edmund Gale's son Edmund and Mr. John Waldron, Mr. James Smith, and Mr. John Stone came to learn the art of him, and by that means I got so much acquainted with them that they would persuade my father to let me go to sea with them, and they carried it so far as to get Captain Gale to speak to my father, and he concluded to let me go with them. The snow [*Diligence*] was built and taking in her load of fish at Boston bound for Bilbao, as then it was a time of peace with Spain. And parents made preparation for me to go the voyage, and on the 24 day of September I sailed for Boston, and the same day arrived at Boston His Majesty Ship *Tartar Pink* with the declaration of war with Spain and England.[2] So we were obliged to unload our fish and fix for Cape Fear in North Carolina where we took a load of tar and carried [it] to Bristol, [England,] where all our hands were pressed[3] except our Captain's son, Edmund Gale Junior. From Bristol we went to

---

1 A snow was a small sailing-vessel resembling a brig, carrying a mainmast and foremast and a supplementary trysail mast close behind the mainmast.

2 This was what the colonists termed King George's War, which broke out between England and Spain in 1739. France joined the conflict in 1744, and the conflict continued until the Treaty of Aix-la-Chappelle in 1748.

3 Impressment or pressing was the practice by which British sailors could be seized and compelled to serve in the Royal Navy. In time of war, press gangs scoured British seaports and swept up thousands of sailors to man its many vessels, and these forcibly (sometimes violently) conscripted hands were required to serve in the navy for the duration of the conflict. Colonial seaports possessed some exemption from impressment (though the Navy always contested and occasionally ignored their privileges) and its incidence varied enormously from region to region around the empire. Most seamen hated the press. Some protested it openly, and most of the rest dodged it wherever possible.

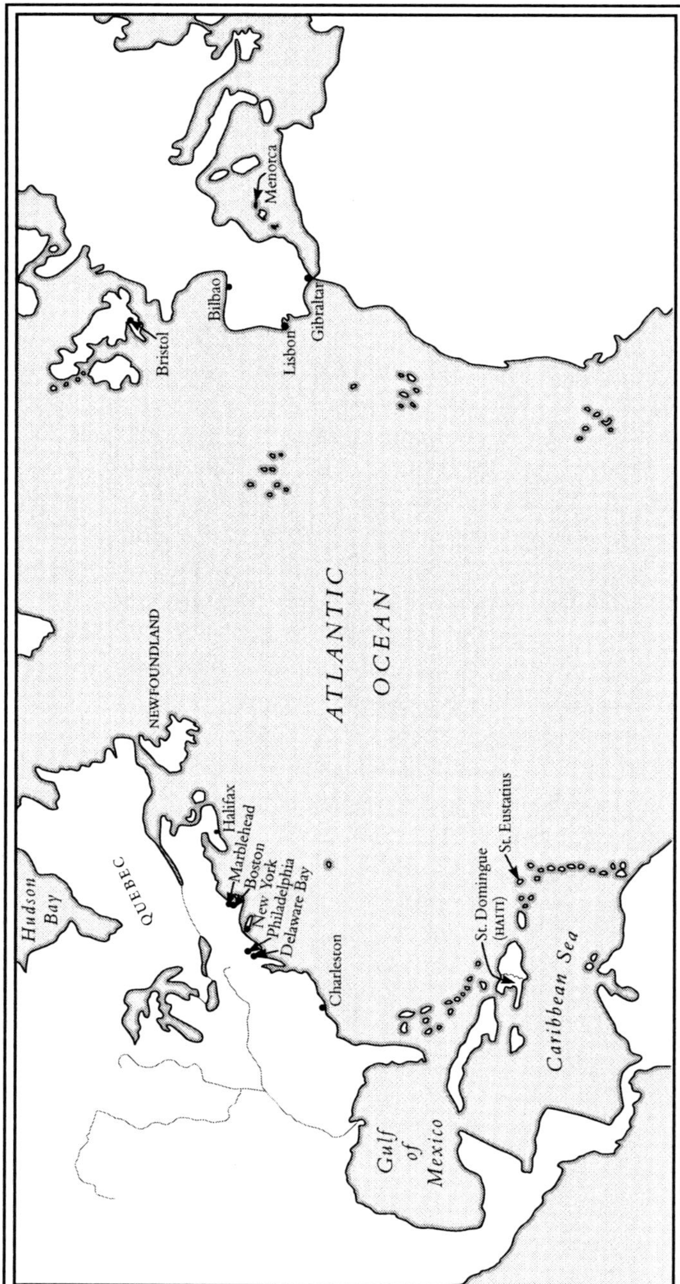
Hudson Bay
QUEBEC
NEWFOUNDLAND
Halifax
Marblehead
Boston
New York
Philadelphia
Delaware Bay
Charleston
ATLANTIC OCEAN
Bristol
Bilbao
Lisbon
Gibraltar
Menorca
St. Domingue (HAITI)
St. Eustatius
Caribbean Sea
Gulf of Mexico

Swansea in Wales and took in a load of coals and came home. Arrived at Boston in August. Then I inclined to go to school this fall. My brother Edward sailed with Captain Gideon Ball in a ship for London and was impressed, and in October my mother died, which was the greatest part of my ruining as may be seen the year following.

1741

This is the hardest winter as any now in America have ever seen. Early this year my father went a-suiting to Mistress Hannah Harris, a fine rich widow. To obtain his wish he would separate his own family or anything else. When our mother died, she left nine children—one an infant; Edward, on board a man-of-war; Mary, a young woman who had the care of our family; Nathan, a ship's cousin;[1] poor I, a hardy lad to stand all brunts in behalf of the rest, for my father took care to keep the shore aboard by a good fireside, and Nathan with him. We at home had neither wood nor food but what I should fetch from Mrs. Harris's, and so I fit the remaining part of this winter. And in April come a snow from Boston consigned to Captain Tasker, and, as hands was very scarce, Captain John Stacey and Captain John Tasker recommended me to Captain Peter Hall as an apprentice to him. And Mrs. Harris had a son named Nathaniel which had been a voyage to sea, and my father and his mother said that we two would lessen their family much if they were both bound out. And Mrs. Harris bound Nat to Jacob Fowle, a house carpenter, and my father bound me to Hall. I was bound April the 15, witness John Stacey and John Tasker. After I was bound, my master said two shifts of apparel would be sufficient for me, but with difficulty I got that, and so I came off an apprentice at 13 years and three month old.

Note: I was bound the 15 of April to Captain Peter Hall of Boston to serve him seven years. He then commanded a fine snow called the *Hawke*, after Captain Edward Hawke, then commander [of] His Majesty's Ship *Portland*, then at Boston and owned by Sir Harry Frankland, a native of England.

---

1 A "ship's cousin" was a rating or an apprentice who berthed aft but whose duties were with the forecastle hands.

We sailed about the first of May and before we got Halfway Rock[1] astern I had a smart rope's ending from my master. O Dear my Mother! We went to Philadelphia and back to Boston ... and when returning [home], we was informed that there was a strong press home, and our captain intended to land our men at Marblehead, but as we got to the Graves it fell flat calm and we came to an anchor and made signals for a boat to come off, and intending to take out three of our men that were liable to be pressed. One coming off saw the man-of-war's barge coming with all fury, [so] she returned again. Then our Captain concluded to try to secrete the men [and] ordered one to hang up his hammock in the cabin. Now, our snow was intended for a privateer and [there were] two press beds in our bulkhead of our cabin for conveniency for our cabin guns. And I took the Captain's bedding out and put in the hammock and the mate's bedding in a cabin in the steerage. And just as the barge come along side I put two of our men in the Captain's press and one in the mate's press, and, as the doors hung up, after the men were in I let down the doors and buttoned them. The Captain ordered me to stay below and down came a midshipman[2] and demanded of me, "Where is your men?" I said they were sent ashore at Marblehead in a fishing boat. He ordered me to open our lazarets scuttle,[3] which I did. Then finding [it] all full, he examined our small arms and missing some of our cutlass and pistols out of their places and began to examine our bulkheads. And seeing the hinges and the thickness of our press, [he] looked at the hooks that held up the press door [and] said, "Boy, what are these hooks for?" I said to hang up wet clothes. And then he stooping down to unbutton the press doors, I took him by the skirts of his coat. I said, "Sir, will you have a dram?" He, looking earnest at me, said, "You are a knowing Dog! You may fill me a junk bottle of rum!" I said, "Sir, will you have a lump of loaf sugar?" And he said, "Put it in the boat!" and went on deck. [Then he] said, "There is

1 Halfway Rock was a small domed rock half-way between Boston and Gloucester, east of Marblehead Neck.

2 A midshipman is a non-commissioned naval officer ranking immediately below the most junior commissioned officer.

3 A lazaret or lazaretto was a section of the fore part between decks, in some merchantmen, in which provisions and stores were stowed; a scuttle is a rectangular opening in a deck with a moveable cover.

none to be found on board." So they took two prentices &c. Now, sir, as soon as the barge was gone, I let the safe guard[ed] prisoners out, and they were almost strangled to death being so close confined and two of them very large and bulky [so] that they reflected on being confined but had rather have stood on deck and opposed the press gang. One of these men's names is or was Jacob Hawkins; another is or was Robert Knight, both born in Marblehead. The other [was] Jacob Waters, born in our Charlestown;[1] the two prentices, one named William Clemons [and] the other James Master, and they were both cleared. Note: on our voyage to Phi[ladelphia], my master's wife was delivered of a daughter. And, as Customs Service visitors came &c., one evening came one Mr. Willy Nichols to see my master, he being a neighbor where he formerly had lived near the Old North Meeting House.[2] I coming home from on board, dirty as I was, for if I had a clean shirt I must wash it myself, my master said, "You, sir, serve a glass of wine here!" And as I came to my Uncle Nichols and gave him a glass I smiled and bowed to him. Said Nichols, "Captain Hall, what boy is this?" He said, "It is Bowen, the Lawyer's son, of Marblehead." And said Nichols, "What is his name?" "Ashley," replied Master, and Nichols, recalling the cast in my eye, said, "Captain Hall, will you let him come to see me tomorrow?" Hall said "yes" and Nichols went off saying to me, "Come and see me tomorrow," which I did, and he said if my father would not get me away from Hall he would, for he saw enough, and he wrote to my father on the subject &c.

Now it was in the time of New Lights or [George] Whitefield and Company.[3] As my sister Molly was baptized by Mr. [Simon] Bradstreet some small time before, she then being a member at our Uncle Webb's New North Meeting House,[4] and so she would have me baptized there. My master indulging me to spend the evening with her, she took the opportunity to take me with her to Parson

---

1 Bowens refers here to Charlestown, Massachusetts.

2 "Old North" was the First Congregational Church of Marblehead. Its pastor at the time was the Rev. John Barnard (see Appendix F1).

3 George Whitefield (1714–70) was a powerful evangelist who toured New England in 1740, preaching an emotional revivalist Christianity. Those converted by his message were termed "New Lights."

4 "New North" refers to the Fifth Congregational Church of Boston.

Webb's and fit me to be baptized &c. As we [were] preparing our ship for sea, my master allowed me to go to my sister's as often as I should desire, and in order for my being the better prepared for the business he, Mr. Webb, gave me a book of instructions, and I read it as often as I could find time. At length the day was fixed on that I was to be baptized. Note: my master was not consulted in the business, and it happened that one H. Johnson, being at tea at his acquaintances', happened to hear this discovery that there was to be a grand christening at the New North on Sunday. He being a church-man [he] came and acquainted my master of its being me. He, my master, came home and inquired into the affair and found that I had a book, which he demand[ed]. I shew it to him. He directed to me to take the book and carry [it] to Parson Webb's with his compliments and said I was his apprentice and I should not be christened in his time. So I left the book and came off well satisfied as to christening.

Being now fitted, we came to Marblehead to load for Gibraltar. We sailed and arrived safe and after discharging our cargo we took on board fine red sand for ballast, with some wines [and] some large anchors. [In] October we left Gibraltar bound for Boston. Note: we took on board the common sand which was as the red sand in time glasses, and as we came to the westward and, supposed that we were near our Banks, we prepared our vessel for a winter's course by getting our guns in the hold and our topgallant yards and masts down &c. About the 20 of November we experienced a smart gale of wind at NW. We lay our snow to on Friday night under a double-reef[ed] mainsail and at Saturday noon wore ship and lay on the other tack. Our carpenter, finding the pumps choked with the fine sand, made short boxes of the lower b[oxes?] and bags of the upper boxes and &c. After the carpenter had done all that he could to the pump boxes and sounding the pump [we] supposed all was well. The gale continued all Saturday night and our officers supposed all was well. But at 8 o'clock Sunday morning, as my busin[ess] was to get bread out of the hold and water &c., as the watch was called &c. Mr. Kinney, our First Mate, was a-turning out and I was going down the after hatchway, the wind roaring so we scarce could hear one another, the mate told his dream that he was chased by a number of wild cattle and could not make his escape from them. As soon as I got below [away from] the noise of the wind, I heard the cask in the hold knocking against each other and our vessel half full of water. I got up as quick as possible and said, "Mr. Kinney, I can interpret your dream. Your oxen are our water casks and others are all afloat in the hold and our vessel is half full of water." My mast[er], hearing me, said that was not to be trifled with, and all hands turned out, went to work, and got to bailing with all the buckets, kegs, &c. I attended with bread and brandy till Monday morning. We were 24 hours before we freed her, and then my master ordered all hands on deck and said, "Brothers, you all see the position of our ship. I think [it] fitting to engage a winter's course," and all consented [to m]ake sail for the West Indies, and so we go so we [...]. Note: we must have suffered much if we had not [stowed the] guns and had got them down in the hold; although we had filled all our empty water cask and other cask with sand, our vessel was so light we could not tack to windward no more than an empty barrel. And when we arrived at St. Eustatius,[1] we were fain to be warped in by the Dutch ship.

1742

This spring we lay at St. Eustatius loading with molasses in snow *Hawke*. We had a good passage home [and] arrived at Nantasket[2] in March, where all our men were impressed. Then [we] went to Cape Ann[3] and run our cargo, and after some time we brought our vessel to Marblehead and lay. Our owner being a Collector[4] and his vessel at the same time a-running goods made some difficulty. In May we carried [the] snow to Boston and completed for sea. My father came to Boston but would not get me clear of Hall, so when we got to sea I paid for his visit. Note: we fitted out with all kinds of provisions for the garrison of Gibraltar, and as we entered the Strait we found four cruisers and we beat them all off and got in safe. And we lay here six month and then we went to Port Mahon[5] and sold the

---

1 St. Eustasius was a Dutch colony and a free port in the West Indies.

2 Nantasket lies near the entrance to Boston harbor.

3 Cape Ann to the north of Marblehead was the point from which all vessels outbound from Marblehead or Salem took their departure.

4 A Collector was a Collector of Customs for the British government.

5 Mahon was the capital of Minorca, one of the Balearic Islands in the Mediterranean. It was the site of an important British naval base in the eighteenth century.

rest of our cargo and from that to Cagliari in Sardinia; then back to Mahon again and Gibraltar and home. Note: we sailed from Boston June the 30, 1742 and arrived July 1, 1743. When we returned we arrived at Cape Ann and run our cargo of fruit and wines, and there was a great noise about it as about this time a vessel was informed against and Sir Harry [Frankland][1] was obliged to take notice of her and seized her and the concerned swore vengeance against our snow. And we fitted out but Dall [?] and the best voyage that offered was to Philadelphia and Louisbourg.[2] Note: my master had got the Leghorn Cough and gave it to his wife, and going a winter's course and out of credit and I, myself, an apprentice makes it all look cold, and not much clothing or bee[f?].

1743

We sailed for Philadelphia the last of September and in going up the river some of our hands took the boat and made off, and at town our Chief Mate left. Mr. May then was shipped [and] a Scotchman as Mate, named Crumbe, and my master had so much of the Leghorn Cold that he was obliged to heave down here. And with difficulty we were manned again but we put to sea [with] one Robin Knight, a pilot, for the coast of Cape Breton. We arrived at Louisbourg before Christmas and took two-thirds [of] a cargo of rum and sailed for Gibraltar ... and after getting off the coast, we having a sheep on board, my master had it killed to save his life. And in some days after, the weather being summer-warm, the hind quarters of the meat grew stale, and my master took the hind quarter and divided them, and in doing it he borrowed a slice from one part and put it to the other and had it boiled. On Saturday, it being a fish dinner, my usual way was to get the fish that was left at noon for supper. Accordingly, when I had got supper in order, as I took great delight in fitting for my master [his] supper, it being Saturday night and I had made two large cans of toddy.[3] In those days, I gave the care of the frying pan to a

---

1 Frankland was the Collector of customs for the port of Boston.

2 Louisbourg was a French fort and seaport on Cape Breton Island in the Gulf of St. Lawrence.

3 A toddy is made of rum with hot water and sugar.

Frenchman to take care of till I should go aft and lay the [table] cloth, &c., but when I came forward I found all burnt up.

1744

The beginning of this year I find trouble enough as the supper of my master's was burnt. He called for the meat which I had put away for him at noon, which I brought to him and shifted into another dish. And as I had no supper, I took the two slices as I shifted the meat [as] I was always allowed to do and put the two legs in a clean dish by themselves. And in the morrow, Sunday, my master took physic for the Leghorn Cough, and, after its working, he called for his meat. I hastened as usual to get it, and as he examined the dish he said to me, "Is this all the meat I told you to put by?" I said, "Yes, Sir," not thinking of his being so exact as he never was so with me before. He said again, pointing [his] knife to the dish, "Is this all the meat I told you to put by the last night?" I said the two small slices were so thin and watery-soaked I did eat them as I had no supper else. Then said my master with his hands wrung together, "May God never smile on me if I do not tie you up tomorrow morning and flog you as much as ever you saw a soldier flogged at Mahon!" which was a thousand lash. And my master called for his saucepan and minced up his meat and went on as calm as ever with me, but I knew him to be a Englishman, not, as he hath often said, a New England man [who] promises and never pays. He would always fulfill his engagements with me. And so the day passed on with me, but I made no scruple of my pay on the morrow, I having no back doors to go out of and not a friend on board that would assist me. I did not know what course to take for my escape from the punishment throne, so in the morning watch after the helm was relieved at six—my watch below—I dived down in the hold, there being a tree of small fustic[1] stood against the bulkhead of the lazaret. I unstowed till I found length enough for my body to lay undiscovered, and I hauled the wood in again so qu[iet?] that I was not discovered by any of our people when in pursuit of me.

---

1 Fustic is a tropical American tree that yields a light-yellow dye.

Monday morning. At 7 A.M., my master rung his bell for me, and, as I did not answer, the Mate came to inquire for me but could not find me so my master ordered all hands called and went a-searching for me in the longboat and everywhere I possibly might have got on deck and then ordered lights with lanterns to pass fore and aft the hold. I could have put my hand on them, but they could not see me. So continued till 8 o'clock. Then my master come to the hatchway himself and said, "Ashley, come out and I won't touch you." But I thought that too faint to trust so I lay the[re]. Next came the people and said, "Ashley, come out and your master will not touch you." Then came master again and said, "Ashley, you know me! If I say a thing I will stand to it. Come out and I will not touch you." I was loathe to trust that and lay still. And then the people came and said, "Ashley, for Godsake come out for your master will die!" And then came master himself and said, "Ashley, for Godsake come out and I will not ever strike you again!" Some of our people said that he [Ashley] threatened to go overboard last night. Others said [he] had rather die than bear the beating his master would give him. Now I find by this time the rum cask grew very hard and hunger came on. I thought with myself, what should become of me, for after all if I should worry them out hunger would oblige me to come out for drink and meat. So I began to think to give up. The people came down and said, "Ashley, your master will die if you do not come out!" Then about 12 at noon my master came and said, "Ashley, if you will come out I will give you my word I will not touch you any more!" And I thought better to come out by an act of grace than to hazard any more delays. I said, "Here am I!" and directly our people flew down and hauled the wood away and got me out. And one of them desired me to go and ask my master pardon, which I declined.

Monday noon. As soon as I had got into the steerage I saw my master on his knees at prayer on the stern locker. I went into the cabin and he looked at me and said, "How could you serve me so?" I said I knew that he would beat me as he said. He said, "Make me some toddy!" Accordingly, I made it and gave it him, and so on till dinner. All that day quite mild, but the next day, after I had killed a pair of fowls, master chose to gut them, and, after washing his hands, he asked for a clean towel. I had ½ dozen of towels cut from a piece of osnabrigs,[1] but I had but 2 hemmed and both them foul. I went to his chest to get a new one. As I was in haste, I put a foul one in between the gripes and [the] longboat so the roll of the vessel caused the fowl to fall out on deck, and, finally, it washed out of the scuppers. My master, seeing it, stepped down to me and took me by the hand and said now you should not run away from him and brings me up on deck and orders the Boatswain to get two seizings[2] of spun yarn, and I was tied to the rail by each wrist and my trousers let [down] about my heels and my frock tucked into my collar. The Cook was ordered to get a bowl of pickle from the beef cask; my feet [were] tied to the fife rail[3] and master would take his cat with 9 parts of log line[4] and give me a dozen strokes on my back; then take his hand full of pickle and pat it on my back; then take his quadrant and look for the sun; then took a tiff of toddy, and so regularly he would do that office, one after another, till the Mate interfered for me and said if I should die on the passage out he would be a witness against him. He said he would do it till I should cry, for I could not cry, so I spit on my shoulder and wet my eyes and was let go.

So my master and I stood it the rest of the passage until we arrived at Gibraltar, and as he was a man so well acquainted in luxury and a noted Mason, he must make as grand show as possible of his abilities. Soon after we arrived, my master made an entertainment and invited a good family on board as a visit, and, as he frequently lodged on shore at every port, so he coming on board, desired me to scour the paint work in [the] cabin and windows, and all fell in for company the 3d day after. Accordingly, I took soap and sand and scoured the paint and cleaned the windows and glasses &c. and did all I could to make the best appearance I could, and got all dry. But the 2d morning my master came on board, and, after his examining all the cabin and glasses &c., he saw one of the towels, as I had cleaned the windows with [one], and said, "You Rascal! Is this one

1 Osnaburg was a kind of coarse linen (and later cotton) cloth, used especially for making rough hard-wearing clothing, or for furnishings, sacks, tents, etc.

2 Seizings were pieces of yarn or light cord used to bind two ropes or parts of a rope together.

3 Fife rails formed the upper fence of the bulwarks on each side of the quarter-deck.

4 A log line was a thin line attached to the log, which was a thin block of wood loaded so as to float upright in the water and used for ascertaining the rate of a ship's motion.

of my towels?" I said I was forced to take it to clean the glass with and immediately upon it, he, for his word's sake, would not strike me himself, called the Boatswain[1] to tie me up by my two thumb at a staple in the cabin. As we were so nigh [to] the New Mole he thought not to take me to the rail. So the Bosun did and gave me the hint to cry out, but the master of Masonry came in upon us and takes the cat out of the Bosun's hands and took the lines in his hand and struck me with the rope on my back [so] that I have thought that I have felt it ever since. After his passion was over with me, for he durst not afr[...] at the Scotchman his mate ill, so all was laid on poor Ashley's back. So, after master was gone on shore, my old friend Mr. Thomas Ling's launch come on board for some what as we had sundries to sell on board. So I laid in with the crew.

This evening, when Mr. Ling's launch returned on board, I concealed myself in her and when I got on board there I made my application to Mr. Ling and he took me into his berth and the doctor messing with him.[2] The doctor desired to see my back and Mr. Ling entertai[ned] me all night, and next morning the doctor went on shore, and some time after I saw our yawl come on board the chebec[3] with the doctor and my master. And coming along side I handed the rope to my master which said to me, "Sir, you have got a bigger ship for your money!" I answered, I hoped so. Then my master asked for the Commanding Officer, which [was] the left-enant, and master was demanded aft and then came forward again and ordered my things into the yawl, and Mr. Ling and the leftenant had some words but Mr. Ling could not prevail to keep me on board. So I went on board snow *Hawke* again, and when I came on board I found a French cook and poultry and bread &c. So my master thought to make me as great an example as [possible and] he ordered me to be lashed by my two thumbs and to hang across the rig rope of our awning without trousers or breeches. The yawl being gone after two gentry and when they came on board [and] saw me in that posture, the woman cried out, "Captain Hall, for Godsake let us go on shore again on a Christian land!" With that, my master

1 A boatswain, or bosun, is the officer in a ship who has charge of the sails and rigging.

2 At sea, messing with someone is to take one's meals with the person.

3 A chebec or xebec is a small three-masted vessel common in the Mediterranean. A yawl is a small ship's boat, usually with four or six oars.

ordered me to be took down, but the company would not stay to eat any of the Frenchman's cookery and all hands of them returned on shore again, master and all. So good.

May. Laying at Gibraltar in the New Mole,[1] so called. Came in the *Solebay* with a Spanish ship, and the prize hauled in to New Mole. We lay alongside of her so our Mate and people all went shares in the plunder—that the men-of-war's men called plunder—and we got a good deal of riches. Then came a 60-gun ship bound for Mahon, and we sailed under her convoy and arrived safe at Mahon and landed our cargo of rum, and there we found letters for us not to return home to New England till the cry was over, for the people swore there they would destroy [our] vessel and cargo. So my master thought to get her into the King's Service [as] a transport, but as she was single-decked he could not get her in. And a brig belonging to Boston cast away on the island [so] my master shipped the captain—his name is Blaney—[as] master of our snow *Hawke* to go to Cagliari[2] and get a load of salt and then to Boston. And she did accordingly. And my master keep me and the snow's yawl with him at Port Mahon, and my master was determined to be a merchant and bought sundry kind of stores accordingly, and I kept store and he hired a house, and we keep house and store, and for a Mrs. I had 21 for wisling [?] for and some soldiers' wives; he would lend 3 half johannes[3] at a time and his wife possibly not 3 pence Sterling, [she] suffering at Boston, New England. Note: my master's wife was Elizabeth Kinney, a daughter to Mr. Benjamin Kinney, sister on mother's side to Colonel [...] Carnes, a brazier at Boston, but much reduced. I was not bound to my master's wife with himself, and now, keeping store at Mahon, I of course was acquainted in the land affairs as well as sea. So I did my endeavor to please both as my master was a Free and accepted Mason [and as] I had a great opportunity to inform myself of both as much as my capacity would allow me. So I made it my study to conform to the Will of God.

At Port Mahon. September and October I was employed attending store. Note: we sold Liverpool potatoes by the quint[al][4] and, as we had porter in bottles, loaf sugar and brown and so [forth] by retail,

---

1 The New Mole was one of Gibraltar's harbors.

2 Cagliari is the capital of Sardinia.

3 Johannes were Portuguese gold coins.

4 A quintal is a hundredweight or 112 lbs.

a soldier came for ½ quintal of potatoes and, having nobody to assist me, a large hogshead having some potatoes in it, I stooped [into] the cask and lay the whole of my body on the chime of the cask. And [as] I was getting the potatoes, my master came in and saw me in that situation and, having an exceeding large cane, he gave me [so] many smart blows on the small of my back that I could scarce get home. I made complaint to the General but [got] no relief. Another time he at me with his cane across my face. He broke the bridge of my nose. Then he would punch at me with his [cane?] in my stomach or anywhere he could come at best &c. Note: after the snow returned from Cagliari he would not let them have product for fear the Mate and people would leave her and bribed the product master till the convoy was ready, and she sailed for home crippled as she was, for she carried away her foremast and shipped it again, new stepped at the partners, and reef[ed] foresail, but my master sent his picture home to his wife and some effects else, but did not pay any of the people their wages. Note: the first part of this year the Spanish fleet got out of Toulon[1] and a French fleet came out with them, and as an English ship would go to engage a Spaniard a French ship would run between them to take the fire from the English. So the French got the Spanish ships out of their port, and Admiral [Thomas] Mathews had the supreme command, although the inferior officer for Old [Richard] Lestock was a man of war from his youth, and between them both [the] Spanish fleet got off and the French into Toulon, &c.

At Port Mahon. December. One evening as I left our store I came to Mrs. Wallace's to see if my master was there, as I frequently did every evening when leaving our store, and I found my master and Mr. Preston, a Church of England clergyman, Chaplin to the Army, and my master said that "This lad of mine was never christened." The parson asked my master if he was sure of it. He said he was for "he intended to have been christened after he was bound to me, but I prevented it." Then the parson asked me if I would be christened. I said if it could be done with sincerity I should be glad. Then the parson asked my master if I could read. He said I could and that I knew the church service well. The parson said it might be done if the lad chooses. Mrs. Wallace asked me if I would accept of her as a

---

[1] Toulon was France's major naval base in the Mediterranean.

godmother and my master asked me if I would accept him as a godfather, and a Mr. Paton asked me if I would accept him as another godfather, to which I agreed, and Mr. Preston desired me to wait on him at his house soon in order to be examined, and I went and afterwards it was agreed to be done on the Eve of Christmas. So my master and my godmother both prepared a cake each. Note: the cake was four pounds of flour, four pound of loaf sugar, four pound of butter, and two dozen of eggs, the yolk only, and beat up well, and they tried, which shouldst be the best, and, on the day before the time, my master wrote bills to Admiral, to General, to Captains of the soldiers, to Captain of the Navy, to merchants, to all men of n[ote?], and to a Romish Bishop and a priest, about 33 [in all]. My master prepared a fine suit of clothes new.

December the 24. This day our matters were all fitted for the evening and at dark the room was furnished with guests and then came on the ceremony, and I was christened by the name of Ashley and signed by the sign of the Cross in token that hereafter &c. And after the ceremony was over, one merchant by the name of Green took his hat and put a guinea in it and went round the room and collected 19 dollars and one real of plate and brought [them] to me and said, "Here, take this. [It] is your own and make good use of it as an encouragement for you!" And I took care of it. Two large cakes, a fine large English cheese with many sorts of wine, rack punch, rum ditto, and brandy ditto in a large upper room. So finish the christening and year 1744.

1745

This is a year of trouble for me, all but death. The first part was spent mostly a-masquerading and &c. I was employed keeping store and attending my master &c. The largest ships were all boot-topped[1] and some hove down.[2] We sold a great deal of rum, but rum being in much demand [and there being] a fine well of fine water in the bounds of our store, my master would employ me in dodging off 10 or 12 gallons

1 Boot-topping was the act of cleaning the upper part of a ship's bottom, and daubing it over with a coat or mixture of tallow, sulphur, or resin.

2 Heaving down was to turn a ship over on one side by means of purchases attached to the masts, for cleaning or repair.

of rum out of a 60-gallon cask and filling it with water. And so we go on, and my master thought it most to his advantage to victual on board His Majesty Ship *Dorsetshire* with the leftenants and officers, so I was enrolled on board the *Dorsetshire*. [...] I rubbed on till March. Note: His Majesty Ship [*M*]*arlborough* of 90 guns was run down keel out by hand.

At Port Mahon, an apprentice to a P. Hall. As the fleet were all now a-fitting out, my master could not be allowed to keep on board the *Dorsetshire*. I was forced to shift as we could about our dinners as provisions were scarce and company plenty. We did as we could; oftentimes more company than good, &c. As there was more demand for rum, and ours almost gone, my master had sold nearly the last tierce to a native, he made me draw off 15 gallons of rum and fill the tierce with water, and [it was] done by candlelight and the stones of the well was of chalk. My clothes was so dirty I could not well be seen in that dress, so my master gave me a smart trimming that I could not put up with. And His Majesty Ship *Rupert*, Captain [John] Ambrose, lay at St. Phillips, bound to Alexandria, and Mr. Richard Pollard [was] a midshipman on board. I conclu[ded to make] the attempt of leaving my master at Mahon, and the next night I packed all my duds and waited off for St. Phillips and found a man with a boat, and I hired him to put me on board the *Rupert*. And when I came on board I found Mr. R. Pollard and he said he would acquaint the Captain as soon as he returned on board. Note: the Captain of the *Rupert* was gone on board Admiral [William] Rowley for orders and [to] take his leave. And the ship's barge came alongside on one side. My master came alongside with his yawl on the other side. And [with] the ship with her 3 topsails atrip[1] and a peak on her anchor, my master demanded me of Mr. Pollard and I was delivered up to my master.

As my master and I came over the side of the *Rupert*, she broke ground and filled away for sea, and my master ordered the boat's crew to go alongside the *Dorsetshire*. And when on board, he asked Mr. Griffith to let the Boatswain's Mate bring me to a capstan bar[2]

1 When sails are atrip, they are hoisted, sheeted home, and ready for trimming.

2 The capstan is a mechanism, working on the principle of the wheel and axle, on a vertical axis, the power being applied by movable bars or levers inserted in horizontal sockets made round the top, and pushed by men walking round, whereby the apparatus is made to revolve and wind up a cable round its cylinder or barrel; it is used especially on board ship for weighing the anchor or for hoisting heavy sails.

in order to frighten me, which was done, and Captain Burrish, walking his quarterdeck, the people called out "flogging on board." Some left their stations and others, making uproars, Captain Burrish wished to know the meaning [and] sent for Mr. Page, the First Leftenant, which said that Mr. Griffith was the author of it. Then Mr. Griffith was sent for and had a smart repremand for his conduct, and so I was released and sent out of the *Dorsetshire*. And as we came to Mahon, he said he would send me to school and he would never strike me more. So I went to school for a fortnight and then he could do nothing without me. About this time, came in a fine prize ship, taken by the fleet, a ship bound to Martinique from Marseilles [and] taken off Cape de Gata,[1] [which had] run into the whole fleet. Leftenant Fraser of the *Burford*, prizemaster, came to our house and gave the ship so good a character that my master bought an eighth part of [the] ship and cargo and fitted her out for the West Indies. And we sailed in June under convoy, and we arrived at Gibraltar and sailed again under convoy and [had a] 28 day's passage from Gibraltar to St. Eustatius. Note: a few days before we arrived, master gave me a smart trimming and I swore I would leave him.

On board the ship *Strange*, Peter Hall, master, laying in St. Eustatius Road, belonging to Port Mahon. As I came to St. Eustatius, I found several of my acquaintances—Captain William Orne, and others. Note: Captain John Shannon of Marblehead died here and one James Biles was [his] mate and of course became master. And Captain Orne and others advised me to quit the ship [and] come home to Marblehead. As I was taken sick, I was put to sick quarters and I got somewhat better. My master went to St. Christopher;[2] and, as I supposed Biles to be nearly ready, I took all the clothes I had out of the ship and put them in a bag and set off for Biles's schooner on a Saturday night. But as she was not so ready for sea, I was forced on shore again with Biles's promise to take me off again. And in the afternoon he would neither bring my clothes on shore to me nor take me off, so [I] was in a fine box, &c. Biles's boat was ashore several times, but they would not take me off and finally they put to sea with my clothes and all, a gale of wind coming on. And

1 Cabo da Gata is on the southern coast of Spain.

2 St. Christopher, or St. Kitts, was a British island in the West Indies.

I have not any clothes from the ship. I could have wished the Devil had Biles and Orne before that I had harkened to them, but [I was] in fear of my master's coming down from St. Kitts. As it happened, there was an English privateer in the Road. I entered on board her and so got off with what duds I had. As soon as we got on board the privateer, we came to sail. Bright moonlight. We saw a sail coming down from St. Kitts, and we stood for her [and] found her to be my former master, Peter Hall. We let her pass and stood all night on a wind to the SE-ward. This sloop is the *Bumper* of Montserrat, Michael Beesley, commander, 6 four-pounders &c.

I was determined to leave my master Hall as he hath left his wife at Boston. I suppose that he could not have held me as he was bound to learn me and to treat me well. I took this opportunity to try the title and so left him to shift without me. Note: as the privateer was going down to Eustatius, she took the carpenter off a ship with her, and she took a French sloop and sent her in to Nevis,[1] which caused her to return to Nevis again. When she arrived, the captain of the ship put the captain of [the] privateer in prison for carrying away his carpenter. Well then, what must I do, for my master would pursue me to Nevis. So Captain Beesley hired a shallop[2] to go to Montserrat. I asked him to let me go with him, and he gave me his consent, so I went to Montserrat where I found a sloop belonging to Philadelphia, Peter Bostick, m[aster]. I asked him for a passage with him to Philadelphia and he granted it, and I came to Philadelphia. Note: Mr. [...] Harris, a supercargo, died at sea and I attended him and took care of his clothes and was well treated for it. And after I got to Philadelphia, I ship again with Captain Bostick for Charlestown[3] and Jamaica. I was well treated by both the owners. One was Solomon Fussell; the other, John Norwood.

We sailed for Charlestown and arrived safe and took in a freight of rice and sailed for Jamaica, but we were taken on the 10 of January 1746. The sloop's name was *Susannah and Mary*, after the owners' wives. So ends the year 1745, and 1746 begins with new trouble.

---

1 Nevis is another British island in the West Indies.

2 A shallop is a small, single-masted vessel.

3 Charlestown was Charleston, South Carolina.

We sailed from Charlestown December the 27, 1745, and January the 2 we saw some of the Islands and [we] run on all day and at night hove to for fear of the Keys.[1] And on the 3 of January, we were taken by a French privateer schooner [commanded by] an Irish rebel leftenant, and we were carried in to Petit Goâve[2] in Hispaniola, and our Captain and but myself were stripped, the people stripped as naked as they were born. I lay in with one of the people and save[d] all that I had on except one new shirt, which the man gave me two pistareens for, and I was fain to distribute all but one shirt and trousers to my shipmates—[it] was all that I had.

This is another dark year for me, for I was taken by an Irish Frenchman, and after we brought to, our Captain and two hands went on board the schooner in our boat, and the Irishman, Monsieur LeGrand, and 4 Frenchmen came on board us, and I, [to] be sure, came to be a linguist for our Mate. And as our Mate was much frightened, he said, "Jack, I have two dollars by me. I would give them to him!" I said, "Damn him! I would not give them to him!" He said, "Do give them to him!" and I mustered up all my French and said to the leftenant, "Mosher La Pilote Jen a Dwo peasea. S you Wolle pruney Le Wite. A dona Vou." The French Irishman [said], "S Boon Gosson Commesay Urion Jaro moy Wolled Rturney." Our Mate said, "Jack, you speak French!" but the Irishman spoke better English. Then I takes out my silver buttons out of my sleeves and gave [them to] him and he promised me to return them to me again. So we arrived safe to Petit Goâve, and at the first time I saw Captain Bostick on shore I saw him and Mr. LeGrand a-talking in English, so I thought I did not need to speak French, and I asked him for my buttons in English and he said that he should go to Leogane[3] tomorrow and get his gold ones and then he would return me mine. But the next news I heard of him was that he was hung at the Admiral's fore-yardarm as a rebel, or to be.

And we were all ordered to an outhouse as a prison and some

1 The Keys are the Florida Keys.

2 Petit Goâve was a seaport in the southern part of the French Caribbean colony of St. Domingue (now Haiti).

3 Leogane was another port in St. Domingue, just east of Petit Goâve.

niggers as guards over us. There were 51 prisoners when we came, and one died of a day every day till we left the place. Our allowance was 1 pound of bread a day and one pound of salt beef per day and nothing else, so we live and died. The French steward was allowed one pound of beef a man, but he would serve 3 pound to 4 men, bad as it was. And Commodore Macklemar, an Irishman by trade, was the Commander-in-Chief, and he came to see us, and our people chose me spokesman, and I complained of our beef and he chastised the steward. There being compla[ints] of the doctor, he was chastised also. Afterwards, I was taken sick myself, and the doctor took notice of me and sent me a dose that I never got clear of till I had the small-pox. So I had the fever and ague[1] every other day and was twice laid by as dead but come to again, as the niggers were ordered to examine for the dead every morning, and if any that were supposed to be dead and were not given up [by] the rest, [they] were to go to as close prison, and I believe there one or two were buried that might have lived. And so I lived, almost starved for some soft food.

On Easter Sunday I was at the Island of Hispaniola a prisoner, and my discovering my cat was the greatest means of my recovery of my health. On Easter Sunday, I thought to go down into the town, and I set out to walk, and at length I came in sight of the Church, but God in his providence ordered me to a house where was two shady trees, and I sat down at the door and soon discovered my cat and called her to me and she came. And an nigger belonging to the house said "Master, do not hurt that cat." I said that the cat was mine and I should take great care of [her] and [...] and was well pleased. After Church, as I sat with my cat on my shoulder, the master of the house came from Church and said to the nigger, "Why do you let the cat out?" The nigger answered he [Bowen] was the owner of the cat, and when his dinner was ready he ordered a plate, knife, and fork and sent me a plate and a large tumbler of wine and water, and I made a fine dinner and I returned home a new man to my distressed brethren. The next morning the nigger came for me to go to his master and I went, and he desired me to pick out some fish out of a hogshead. And so I stayed all day and at night I returned home with some provisions for my messmates. And so the merchant

1 The fever and ague almost certainly refers to malaria.

treated me all the time till the cartel came and when I came away he gave me sea stores and wished me well. And all for my cat.

After the cartel sailed, we fell in with the *Merlin*, sloop of war, which took 19 men out. I looked so sickly they would not take me, so I got safe to Kingston, Jamaica, where I found Mr. John Norwood, our former owner of sloop *Susannah and Mary*, and I was kindly received by him and sent on board a brig in the [...]. Note: my brother Nathaniel Goodwin was here and would have me to go home with him, but Mr. Norwood chose my going home with him, and I stayed on board the brig and came to Philadelphia a sick man, but my having the fever and ague so much that I could not get a voyage and stayed all summer at Philadelphia. I got some insight at rigging.

May. I arrived at Philadelphia in brig *Dolphin*, Francis Shores, master, owned by Mr. John Norwood, and I was so ill with the fever and ague I could not get a voyage anywhere and no New England men [were] here. As the brig's rigging was not tallied, I getting acquainted with a young man, a rigger, and he got me to work with them as I knew the ropes as they were unrove. And I was employed some time in the rigging loft, and I got so in debt that I was fain to go to work with a plasterer and agreed to serve him three year. And it happened that my intended master and his brother were in partnership and my master was the youngest brother, and there was a day set for a Thanksgiving and the day before I was ordered home by my master to get wood and go off [on] errands. But the oldest brother said I must go for him first. My master ordered me to go for him first, and there was a very great dispute about it, but I said I could not serve them both. So I set off for home, and as I was going home I saw a schooner coming up the river, belonging to Salem. I did what my intended mistress desired me to do but would not go to my master's brother's house, and in the evening the two brothers came home and had a great dispute on my serving them both. My master said I should be bound to him alone and his wife insis[ted I] be bound the next week. But on Thursday, or Thanksgiving day, I went on board the schooner where I found some acquaintance, and the captain said that he knew my father and would take me home and lend me what money I should want. The next morning, both brothers came for me to go to be bound to them both, and it proved very good to me for I had a good opportunity to get clear of both.

And when the schooner [was] ready, I got money and paid my landlord and came home.

October. I left Philadelphia in schooner *Abigail*, Josiah Kellog, master, and arrived at Salem in a fortnight, where I find my father and family all well. And my father paid Captain Kellog what money he had paid for me at Philadelphia, and I stayed at home but a little while before I was shipped by Captain George Jackson to go to St. Eustatius in a sloop [*Richard and William*] that two young men had bought to make a drogher of.[1] Note: there was an express from Annapolis Royal[2] that a fleet of French men-of-war were at Chebucto, now Halifax, and was bound for Boston but sickness dis[s]ipa[ted? them] and they were all dispersed and lost. None returned to France.

November. I sailed with Captain Jackson about the first of November and was taken the 19[th] by two French privateers. I was taken with Captain George Jackson from Marblehead for Eustatius in a sloop that two men belonging to Eustatius [owned], and we were in sight of St. Christophers when we were taken by two French sloops, and John Adams and myself [were put] on board a sloop and cruised in her 13 days and then [were] put on shore at St. Eustatius. And as I had not clothes sufficient to engage a winter's coast, I was advised to sail with Jonathan Burchall, a native of Bermudas, but sailed from St. Croix, a Danish island. And as I was going through the tavern my master Hall came with a file of soldiers after me, but I escaped to the back and got off clear. I shipped myself on board a Danish sloop [*Betsey*], Jonathan Burchall, master, belonging to a Mr. Anson at Basiend [*sic*], St. Croix, where I became a Dane and sailed from there about 6 month.

1747

I sailed in the Dane service till June and then I find passage for Marblehead in schooner *Peter and Mary*, George Jackson, master, and I was discharged from the Dane and came home and tar[ried] at home two month. And I was recommended to one Captain Richard James

---

1 Droghers were small, slow coasting vessels of West Indian design.

2 Annapolis Royal was a British town in Nova Scotia on the Bay of Fundy.

to sail in a new ship a-building [for Mr. Thomas Gunter] at Newbury, Mr. John Reed, Chief Mate, and all hands from Marblehead. But my opinion of Captain James was much different from his great recommendation. I went round to Boston in the ship but could not go any further this voyage. He proved himself to be what his real character was, which was Bloody DICK.

I, finding my townsmen to prove so bad, I was determined to go abroad and try strangers, and in October I went to Boston and went up and down from North End to South to find the biggest rogue I could. There was a plenty of voyages offered, but none suited me as well as an Irishman which bore a name of the biggest rogue. His name was John Copinthorne, a Corkcolen.

October. I shipped with Captain John Copinthorne of Bristol, England, [in the snow *Friendship* owned by Mr. Perry, an anchorsmith in Bristol], for Gibraltar, Faro, and Bristol. He gave me three pounds Sterling per month bound to Gibraltar and Bristol, [I] to be discharged at Bristol. I found the best friendship in him as I ever found in an American or Englishman.

1748

I arrived at Bristol in March, and I boarded at Mr. James Perryman's, late of Marblehead, and after I had learnt navig[ation] I was a-coming to Boston as Second Mate of a new ship that should be built for Messrs. Perry and Company, John Copinthorne, master. He paid me 13 guineas, the balance of my wages. But before I could engage with the master of [a] snow that was bound to Boston, came news of peace with France and Spain, so I was forced to lay on my [...] till I had spent the whole of my 13 guineas. So, instead of having 3 pounds Sterling per month to go for Boston, I must give 3 pounds and work my passage besides. I was all to leeward in my pl[ans].

In July, I engaged to sail in the *Brislenton*, [Captain John Widburn], in Devonshire's and Reeve's employ and worked on board by the day till the ship was below the rolems[?] and then put in to pay at 25 shillings per month. We sailed on the [...] of July. And I had the smallpox at sea and that carried off all the poisoned disorders which hung about me from the time I was a prisoner at Petit

Goâve, as I have mentioned before. We arrived at Charlestown in September and lay all winter, and in February 1749 I was discharged.

Now, after laying all winter at Charlestown, I come [to] Marblehead and I had a promotion, but short.

1749

March. I arrived at Salem in schooner [*Swallow*], Captain Thomas Dean, and come to Marblehead, and my father ordered me to board at Mr. Elias Currel's, and I was soon shipped on board the [schooner] *Duke of Cumberland*, and I went to Barbados in her, Archibald Laws, master. I was before the mast, and after our return from Barbados we turned her into a brig and Captain Laws took me [as] his mate, and we went to Louisbourg, and I carried 6 quintals of merchantable May fish as adventure[1] for Mr. Currel to get a tierce of rum for him. And I did get a tierce of rum on his account.

I arrived in October and as our owners, Captain LeGall[ais], Captain Gerry, Captain Watts, and Captain Laws has a sloop now ready for Carolina and wanted all the rum that come in the brig, which was 6 tierces, [they] took mine with the rest and would fain put me off with dry goods for Mr. Currel's and my adventures. But Mr. Currel's insisting on the rum, and they declining giving me it, so my honored father wrote to Captain Laws concerning the rum as my property and insisted on it, so the owners said that my father threatened the vessel as the goods were contraband, and [so they] gave me one barrel of rum for Mr. Currel and I could get nothing for myself and [was] turned adrift although I had shifted my board on Captain Watts's request and boarded at Mr. Simpson Boden's. So much for Marblehead roguery. Note: my first difficulty was, as I found out, that Captain Watts had a difference with Mr. Currel and, he being a Scotchman disaffected with Mr. Currel, came on board the brig *Duke of Cumberland* and asked me to the cabin and said that I should not expect employ if I continued [boarding] in such a family and advised me to go to board at his Sister Boden's, and he would do as much for me as anybody should, and

[1] An adventure was a private speculation.

I adhered to him and left my boarding at Mrs. Currel's to Boden.

November. I ship in snow *Swift*, Captain William Coles, [as] Second Mate. Snow laying at Cape Ann. We sailed from Cape Ann January 15, 1750 and arrived at Lisbon for orders and sailed for Bilbao, and on the 26 of February we came to an anchor to the eastward of St. Anthony's Head in com[pany] with the *Grand Bigonia* and Captain Linch in [a] snow.

1750

February 26. At 4 o'clock P.M., the snow *Swift* and ship *Grand Bigonia* of Bilbao and a snow, Captain Linch, [were] all beating into St. Anthony's, but the gale was so high that we all were fain to clew up our topsails in the squalls, and the ebb tide come out of St. Anthony's. We were all forced to come to an anchor, and about 12 [at] night our cable parted and we let go another anchor and brought up abreast of Captain Linch. The *Bigonia* hoisted many lights and keep firing off signal guns all the latter part of the night and [at] dawning she cut her cables and run ashore at [...] high water [on Laredo Beach] and cut her mainmast away and [bows]prit. At 8 A.M., Captain Linch put [away] for Bilbao and was lost. At 8 A.M. we parted our other cable, and, [there bei]ng no other anchor to let go, we run her ashore. At 11 ditto we run ashore at Laredo Beach.[1]

Memorandum of my sailing in snow *Swift*, Second Mate, Captain William Coles, master, his son William, Chief Mate, from Cape Ann for Europe, 1750. The snow *Swift*, William Coles, commander, on Wednesday, February the 27, 1750 was shipwrecked. Note: this snow belonged to Mr. John Rowe of Boston, ¾ of ship and cargo. The other 4th belonged to Captain Coles, an native of Topsham in England. We sailed from Cape Ann, January the 15, 1750 and arrived at Lisbon and was advised for Cadiz or Bilbao. When off the Rock, the wind being southerly, stood to the northward for Bilbao. On February the 26 this afternoon a smart gale at NW. We tried to get into St. Anthony's, but we could not. We took a pilot for Bilbao [but we] were forced to come to an anchor. Note: the ship *Grand Bigonia*

1 These events all took place near Bilbao on the north coast of Spain.

and Captain Linch in a snow fr[om] Lisbon came to an anchor with us [and] lay all night.

After I was shipwrecked in the *Swift*, I got to Bilbao and there I found some friends, viz. Captain A. Tucker, Kimball, and some Salem men. So I live well and I was advised to go Mate of a schooner to St. Peter's, Newfoundland, William Jameson, master. And [we] sailed from Bilbao [in the schooner *Betsey*] and arrived at St. Peter's, and I went to the Bank a-fishing till the last of September and [I was] then discharged and a bill[1] on Mr. Griffen for my wages got to Boston safe.

At Boston. December. I shipped myself Mate of a sloop [*Friendship*], Captain Christopher Prince, master, for New Bern, North Carolina. [We] sailed the 21 of December [and] arrived at Cape Lookout 25 Jan[?] where I lay all winter. In the spring, came a snow from Jamaica, Joseph Goodwin, master, belonging to Plymouth, New England. As I was off my guard and over-persuaded, I changed with [...] Brimall, Mate of snow [*Commerce*], bound for London.

1751

I sailed for London, Mate of the *Commerce*. Arrived at London July 2. Snow sold. I tarried at London four months. Note: I saw my old master, Peter Hall, late of Boston, and I came from London in the *Nancy*, Second Mate, John Suter [master], at Bordeaux. Christmas Day [we] called at the Grand Canary; from thence to Jamaica, and I was discharged by Captain Gloss. So goes on.

1752

At Jamaica. April. Sailed for Philadelphia in the snow *Betsey*, Abiah Hadaway, master. William Varsell, Esq. and wife and wife's sister [were] passengers, and [the snow was] owned by Squire Varsell. I was a passenger. The carpenter was a cousin of mine and Mr. Greener [Greenough?] married his sister. Note: Greener was Mate, so I fare well, and we arrived at Philadelphia the beginning of May, &c. I

---

1 A bill here was an order for Griffin to pay Bowen his wages.

arrived at Philadelphia, and I was recommended by Mr. [...] Greener to Mr. Noah Bowen to go with him as Sailing Master[1] of a sloop to New York and to Rhode Island at £3 currency per month and [to] Carolina in [the] winter. I went to Cape May and fixed [the] sloop and loaded her at Tuckahoe Egg Harbor, and delivered our load at Wilmington.[2]

October. Mr. Thomas Mulford ship[ped] me to go to Cape Fear with him [as] Sailing Master, and I came to Cohansey with [the] sloop [*Susannah*] and took in a cargo for Cape Fear. A young woman freighted one half of the vessel, by the name of Polly Walling, and we sailed from Cape May. Arrived at Cape Fear and arrived at Wilmington and went up the NE branch as far as Exeter, then to Wilmington, so home. Note: Captain Townsend and crew [came] home with me and all our passengers, men, women [and] ch[ildren].[3]

1753

March. I returned from Cape Fear as above. I was employed this spring in the Delaware River. June. I had a freight for Rhode Island. I went through the Sound[4] by way of New York, back outside Long Island, and so passed the summer season. In September, came a Mr. John Leeke as agent from a company of whalemen to engage my vessel, for me to go master or for me to get any other. So my owners agreed for [the] sloop to go, to be ready by November 20 at Cape May.

November 20. At Cape May. Took on board 12 men and all their appurtenances for whaling and two whaleboats and set out for a whaling voyage. I have £3 currency per month and 2/-1/2 per on oil.[5] We are engaged to attend the men, of March to bring them home again and all their effects.

---

1 A sailing master was one who had responsibility, like a shipmaster, for the navigation and handling of a vessel, but not the conduct of business connected with the voyage.

2 Cape May and Tuckahoe are in New Jersey; Wilmington is in Delaware; and all are on the shores of Delaware Bay.

3 Cohansey, is in southern New Jersey, close to the mouth of Delaware Bay, as are Greenwich and Maurice River (see entries for 1754).

4 The Sound is Long Island Sound.

5 The men were being paid partly by the month and partly in shares of the oil they landed.

I tarried in Cape Fear River all winter. The whalemen at Lockwood's Folly[1] got nothing.

1754

March. Sailed from Lockwood Folly in sloop *Susannah*, with 12 men and all their empty barrels, butts, and appurtenances, but [they] did not get a drop of oil. So I lost nearly £12 currency by supplying one of the men. After we returned to Cape May and landed our people and their stuff, I took our small boat and came to Grinwags [Greenwich]. Our sloop was sold and I discharged. As I have sent many letters to my father and cannot get an answer, I find I cannot get anything. I think I'll go home to my father.

I have tarried here at Cohansey two years and cannot get a letter from my father, although he hath sent me several. I have many friends here and relations, but [they are] not satisfied by my notes [without] a letter from home to prove that I am as I assert to be. Engaged with B. Sears to go to New York, but he sold his sloop also, and I came passenger with one [Josiah] Pool to Maurice River, and [I was] determined to take passage with him home and got my chest ready but could not get my sm[all?] debts in so I came away bare and not well clothed.

I settled all my affairs at Cohansey that I could and sent my chest on for Maurice River, and when my unknown friend John Brick knew of my leaving the town of Greenwich he implored[?] me to tarry and said if I would abide with them he, John Brick, Junior, would build a sloop of such dimensions as I should think fit for foreign trade or coasting and that I should be charged with the one half of the vessel but would not demand any pay till she had earnt. But as my chest was gone I [...].

I left Greenwich the latter part of July and came to Maurice River in the Bay of Cape May, West New Jersey, and set sail for Rhode Island, a passenger, and came to New York and down [Long Island] Sound and arrived at Rhode Island, Josiah Pool master of sloop [*Racehorse*]. When at Rhode Island I went and saw Mr. Eleazer

---

1 Lockwood's Folly is on the Outer Banks of North Carolina.

Trevett, and he had a sloop bound directly to Marblehead and I might have a passage, but I could not settle with Captain Pool for money I had lent him so could not go, and the sloop sailed but returned again this night. So good. I settled with Captain Pool, and the sloop [*Robin*] sailed for Providence Monday morning. I saw Mr. Trevett and he said one of his men had left the vessel and that he would give me wages round to Marblehead. So I came round as a hand and arrived at Marblehead. [I] find my father and his wife and all my brothers and sisters well. I stayed by [the] sloop till she sail[ed] for Rhode Island. After I was acquainted at Marblehead, I found a vacancy for a Mate in Robert Hooper's employ. I sat up for a Mate's berth. I saw Mr. Hooper and offered my service as a Mate, but the answer was "I do not know you!" I said my name was A. Bowen. [He said] "I know that, but as you have been master abroad I do not know your behavior." I applied to Jerem[iah] Lee,[1] and he gave me the same answer and said I must go a voyage before the mast before I should have any employ from here.

I have been out of employ from September till December. Mr. Robert Hooper [was] having a snow a-building at Newbury, and he gave the command to John Russell, and I engaged to go to Newbury with him for her as a foremast man. I went and helped get in her masts and then we rigged her and brought her round to Marblehead in her and I tended her all winter.

1755

About the 12 of March 1755, we sailed from Marblehead in the fine new snow *Halley*, Captain John Russell, master, bound for Lisbon. Arrived at Lisbon in 25 days. Then we sailed for Cadiz, and there I saw Captain Joseph Prince and Captain John Griste in the snow *Champion*. We sailed from Cadiz for Oporto[2] where we discharged our cargo and took salt and came home complete in thirteen weeks.

---

1 Robert "King" Hooper (1709–90) and Jeremiah Lee (1721–75) were the two most prominent fish merchants in late colonial Marblehead and among the richest merchants of any kind in New England. During the American Revolution, Lee was a Patriot and Hooper a Loyalist.

2 Oporto is in Portugal north of Lisbon.

All well. Samuel Colton of Salem was Mate, and left. I supposed the berth belonged to me, but Mr. Hooper referred me to Captain [Joseph] Howard.

August. I shipped [as] Sailing Master for a ship a-building at Boston, Thomas Goldthwait factor for one William Wonza of Bristol, England, to go for Bilbao if no war.[1] To come to Marblehead to lade fish. I went to Boston. Was launched in ship *William* and when completed we sailed for Marblehead on September the 14 where we lay till the last of February when we sailed for Lisbon.

As we were so long in loading after longering[2] that on our passage we ship[ped] a sea and upset all our fish that was longered so much that, not withstanding I had got everything to the windward side, when we arrived at Lisbon with the black strake under water and our larboard side and bends out of water on the other, and we opened the lower hatches and put the hold to rights again. We discharged three of our men here, and I had her to man again, which I soon did, and we sailed for Bilbao and delivered all our cargo of fish safe. Then Captain Howard discharged me and all the crew and gave the carpenter and me 3 month pay to quit the ship, and I took passage with Captain Peter Green in the *Lucretia* for Lisbon, where we arriv[ed].

1756

At Lisbon on board Captain Peter Green. I got to Boston in schooner *Ranger*, Barnabus Binney, master. Then I come to old Marblehead again and tarried in Mr. Hooper's employ till December. Then I shipped mate of Captain Philip Lewis for the West Indies in schooner *Swallow* of Mr. Hooper's.

When I entered on board the *Swallow* it was in the latter part of November when we sailed, and we were taken the 13 December by a John Chavers[?], commander, of Martinique and carried in there. Captain Lewis and myself [were] kept at the merchant's house. Our people were imprisoned. I had all encouragement to get away, which

---

1 The war to come was the Seven Years War.

2 A "longer" is a row of casks stored next to the keelson in order to stabilize the vessel.

I took all the care I could in doing it. I got many of Captain Lewis's shirts and thin clothes away and my own. On Sunday, Captain Lewis, Mr. George Crowninshield, and myself made our escapes on board a schooner and got to St. Eustatius safe, where I find many friend. Note: Captain Lewis took a half Joe[1] off one of the merchants and gave him an order to Barbados. Not good. Mr. James Freeman had bought a sloop, intending her to go to Martinique for a load of molasses and then to Marblehead. He offered the sloop to Captain Lewis but must have a Dutch paper carrier, but Lewis could not undertake this voyage, and he recommended me to Mr. Freeman. So, I went back to Martinique again where I was discovered but well treated by [the] merchant and captains of privateer and officers. I paid the half Joe that Captain Lewis had, and they gave me Captain Lewis's chest and bedding and my chest and all my things, and I went all round the island to get the cargo and got her full and down to Eustatius again, where I hoisted English colors and came home master. The sloop is the *Olive* of St. Eustatius.

1757

Olive. I got home to Marblehead in June. I delivered my cargo according to bills of lading. I being consigned to Mr. Robert Hooper, I was obliged to follow his orders and lay up the sloop till hurricane month were over, and in September I had her [...] and the main deck caulked before the badness was discovered. And when the carpenters opened her sides to shift her beams they found every beam and knees[2] rotten and were obliged to b[uild] all new main deck. And all that took them till November, and I did not sail from home till December. Arrived at St. Eustatius 24 December.

1 The same Portuguese coin referred to in n. 3, p. 47.

2 A knee is a piece of timber naturally bent, used on a vessel to connect the beams with the timbers.

1758

Sloop *Olive* begins this year with me. As the sloop cost so much to repair her, and but an old bottom, at last I concluded to take passage with my brother, [Nathan Bowen,] in the [brig] *Hannah*. So after I had settled all my business with Mr. Freeman I came away with him and went to Anguilla[1] for salt and then home to Marblehead.

Schooner *Betsey* belonging to Deacon Joshua Orne, Michael Coombs, master. I ship [as] his Mate and went to Lisbon and back again. I went one trip a-wooding to Townsend[2] with Abras Mulle [Abraham Mully?] and did not go any more to sea this winter, and I stayed with my wife to see how it would suit to live on shore, and so forth.

After my return home in brig *Hannah*, on the 7 of May I married Miss Dorothy Chadwick of Bradford, daughter to Edmund and Mary Chadwick.[3] The July following, I sailed for Lisbon, Mate of Captain Michael Coombs, and returned in October and I went to the Eastward for wood and I tarried at home all winter.

1759

And the 29 of March 1759, the Honorable Robert Hooper Esq. would have me engage to go on board one of His Majesty's ships of war at Halifax, and he promised me that he would recommend me to the Governor of this Province and to the Admiral or Comman[der] in Chief of His Majesty's ships of war at Halifax.[4]

Mar. 29 This morning I saw the Honorable Robert Hooper Esq., and he asked me to come to his store and I came after breakfast, and he gave me a plan of a proc[lamation] in writing and said there was one gone to be printed. He said that he would have five midshipmen to go out of Marblehead, that our quota of men by our General Courts[5] were 45, and the Courts would have all the seaports to send

1 Anguilla is one of the Leeward Islands of the West Indies and a British possession.
2 Townshend is now Boothbay Harbor, Maine.
3 See Appendix A.
4 This is the first reference to the Quebec campaign of 1759.
5 The General Court was the legislature of the colony of Massachusetts.

their part of the five thousand men which were to be raised to go by sea on board His Majesty's ships at Halifax under Rear Admiral [Philip] Durell and the enlistments to be complete by the 6 of April. After taking my father's advice, I enlisted in behalf of Captain William Courtis's Company. He gave me ten dollars for the Company and Colonel [Jacob] Fowle gave me a Provincial note of twenty dollars and His Majesty's Royal Bounty was forty shillings sterling, and I was the means of enlisting 17 seamen this day. Note: we are to be complete the 6 of April, which we were. I had 32 seamen belonging to the sea department out of 45, the town's quota of the five thousand men that should be raised by our General Courts for the service of this year 1759. Our people were all sent to the Castle[1] but myself, and on the 4[th of April] a schooner came in here for me, and on the 12 we sailed for Halifax, where we arrived the 16, and 16 of my men were ordered on board the *Pembroke* and 16 on board the *Squirrel*, and I had my choice of either ship so I chose the *Pembroke*, John Simcoe, Esq., and I was ordered to walk her quarterdeck as a midshipman and [I] was quartered at the braces. We were in Rear Admiral Durell Division and sailed for Quebec May the 3 with [t]en sail of the line and two frigates [and] 3 transports.

Memorandum of my reception by Captain John Simcoe Esq. [of *Pembroke*] after delivering my letter from Admiral Durell to Captain Simcoe. He said to me, "What country are you of?" I said I was born in Marblehead. "Did you serve your time to the sea?" I said, "Yes, sir." "What trade did you use?" I said, up the Mediterranean. "What part?" I said, "From Gibraltar to Port Mahon and to Cagliari on the Island Sardinia for salt and back to Mahon and home to Boston again." And then Captain Simcoe said, "What principles are you of?" I said of the Church of England. He asked me if we had a Church of England in Marblehead. I said, "Yes, sir." "And was you christened at the church at Marblehead?" "No, sir. I was christened at Port Mahon." "And how came you to be christened there?" I said I never was christened in my youth [and] my master would have me christened. He said, "Who was your master?" I said, "A master of a merchantman and [he] tarried on shore and sent our vessel home to New England, and, as I being an apprentice, keep me with him, and I keep store for him, and as my

1 The Castle was Castle William, a fort in Boston harbor.

master spent the afternoon with the Reverend Mr. Preston I came home from store. My master said that I was not christened, and they concluded to have me christened. And the day before christening my master wrote, [I] expect, 40 bills and sent me to the Admiral and General and to all the captains in the Navy and army and merchants [and] other officers to invite them to the christening." And Captain Simcoe said, "What was your master's name?" I said, "Peter Hall." And he said, "I was one of the guests!" And all well.

Note: this is a list of the people that came on board this ship with me from Marblehead, &c.

[On board *Pembroke*]

William Horn	Thomas Woodfine
Edward Arkis	Miles Dolton
Jonathan Welch	Edward Kinsley
Robert Bartlett	Benjamin Nichols
Garrett Farrell	Arthur Lloyd
John Bateman	Edward Sovering
Isaac Warren	Zach Pain
Frederick Swayer	Robert Thompson

A list of the people on board the *Squirrel*

John Melzard	Samuel Look
Thomas Dove	Francis Mesolte
William Mathews	Roper Linsteed
William Uncal	William Corkering
Samuel Corferin	Charles Jacobs
John Stedman	Walter Stoer
John Goldsmith	Samuel Lines
Thomas Walpy	Thomas Peach

Note: His Britannic Majesty's ship *Pembroke* dimensions were 153 feet keel, 42 feet beam, and 19 feet hold, 6 feet between decks, gundeck 156 feet [and] 12 ports. [The officers were] John Simcoe Esq., commander, who died May 14; afterward John Wheelock Esq., First Leftenant James Norman, an Englishman; John Robson, Second; James Beechenokis [Bechinoe], Third; Mr. James Cook, Sailing

Master,[1] which went on discovery and was killed by savages; our Boatswain's name [William] Thompson; Doctor, [James] Jackson; Gunner, [William Simmonds]; Carpenter, [John] Bevis; Cook, [Henry] Walker; Purser, [Richard] Wise; Mustermaster [Master's Mate, William] Metcalf; [Peter] Napier [and James] Wilson, [midshipmen].

A memorandum of my knowledge of the Immortal Cook. As I happened to be on board His Britannic Majesty's Ship *Pembroke* on the expedition against Canada, Mr. James Cook, our Sailing Master, seeing my plan of The Harbor and City of Halifax which I took [drew] on the 30 of April 1759 when Vice Admiral Saunders came in from England and General James Wolfe[2] came in the *Neptune*. As soon as the *Neptune* had come to an anchor, I walk[ing] the quarterdeck of the *Pembroke*, saw a barge steering for us. I said, "This barge is coming for us!" and as the orders are 4 men for side, four men for side these were placed, and as the Setter [*sic*] came up he said, "Is Captain Simcoe on board?" The answer was "Yes." He paid no compliment to officers, but crossed the quarterdeck and went past the sentry into the cabin. And when Mr. Norman, our First Lieutenant, saw the surprise he inquired of the coxwain which was coming up the gan[gway], "Who is this gentleman that so came on board?" "General Wolfe!" "Call the Sergeant [of] Marines! Call the Boatswain! Call the Master-at-Arms! Six clever fellows for side! A file of Marines! Drum and fife!" After all this ceremony, General [Wolfe] I believe he stayed with Captain John Simcoe upwards of half an hour. When coming out, a ruff was beat, side manned, and all well.

June 9 I went with our Sailing Master in our cutter a-sounding for the channel through the Traverse.[3]

June 14 Was sent a boat from our ship and one from the *Devonshire* and another on the easternmost rocks of the Traverse and the other on the westernmost, one with a white flag and the other with a red, and having a leading wind, we all came to sail and run through the Traverse.

---

1 This is the first reference to James Cook, the Pacific explorer. Bowen made little reference to Cook in the journal he kept at the time, but he dwelt on him at length in this autobiography written after Cook's achievements in the Pacific and death in Hawaii.

2 General James Wolfe commanded the expedition against Quebec.

3 The Traverse is slightly downstream of the Ile d'Orléans in the St. Lawrence River below Quebec. Bowen is pulling this reference out of his memory because he was accompanied by James Cook.

June 27 After we had moved and secured our ships, the French annoyed us with some random shot, but their forts was not discoverable. We were fain to fire at random, seeing no object to [aim at] but they cause us to shift out of their way, and so we shifted up and down the River of St. Lawrence till the 27 of June and then we had something to do. We were the first ship of the line that opened Quebec and anchored in the Basin and saw four large frigates and three smaller laying off the town, and, it was said, that the French had given up the idea of fighting with them and had converted them all into fire ships.[1] The French had two large floating batteries of eight squares, two 18 pounders in a square and a sail or mast in the center and a yard of 60 feet. And one of them was so near us that we could have talked together, but they seeing our lower deck guns run out and the wind to the eastward, they let down their sail and was hauled up to the mouth of [the St.] Charles River[2] and there moored as a safeguard for that river.

And at the ebb of the tide, we hove up and went to backing and filling down the river. I being quartered at the braces, our Master, Mr. James Cook, ordered me to the poop to command the main yard by the braces, and he requested the Lieutenant of the Royal American soldiers to send me 50 men to assist me with the brace, and the Lieutenant ordered Sergeant Arnold to see the men there, and we backed and filled[3] down there. Note: General Wolfe landing at the same time on the body of the island of Orleans and a smart gale of wind which did much damage to our fleet. I hove the log and the tide run nine knots by us. What a piece of work!

June 29 This night at 12 o'clock I saw a falsefire[4] above. I went down and acquainted Mr. Norman him that the fire ships were a-coming down and when I came up again there was seven ships on fire from their topgallant mastheads [to] below their bends and out at their yard arms. O what a dismal sight! We had 40 boats alongside and were all ordered to assist them in towing them ashore—3 on our starboard side and 2 on our larboard and two sunk above us so none of them did us any damage.

---

1 Fire ships were vessels set on fire to drift down upon the enemy and ignite them as well.

2 The St. Charles River flows into the St. Lawrence just downstream from Quebec.

3 Backing and filling is alternately to back and fill the sails.

4 A falsefire was a blue light produced by combustible material and used as a night signal.

July 6 Admiral sent his boat a-sounding opposite the falls[1] on the island of Orleans and Mr. Cook took me with him in our pinnace.[2] And we had a sounding line and a stand for our brass compass and Mr. Cook sat an object upwards of a mile distance and a stick was set on the end of the line and two men carried the reel and after that we had one length of the line, Mr. Cook said to me, "Bowen, take up a stone," and I did, and then we run another line out and we took each a stone again. The French a-firing shot at us from the North Shore all the time. So we did till we had run eight lines out and Mr. Cook asked me how many stones I had and I counted them and found 8 and he said, "I have 8." Then come a shot so near as hove up the dirt on our clothes so we retreated to [our] boat safe, but the Admiral's boat was so close pursued that the enemy wounded one of the men and carried him off.

July 7 Note: I could not have time to borrow Mr. Wilson's journal book to copy from and Mr. Cook took my book and got his scribener to wre [write?] and he wrote two months in it for me, or from the 7 of July to the last of August. Then I was forced to do as I could.

Memorandum: on July the 15, 1759, according to my journal, our longboat and pinnace was sent to land artillery, and I was sent to assist the longboat in the pinnace, and when we arrived at the place below the Falls of Montmorency we were obliged to ground the longboat for the soldiers to get their cannon out, and we rendezvoused on board the *Porcupine* sloop of war. Our Master's Mate, Mr. Napier, having the command of the longboat, said to me, "Mr. Bowen, I am acquainted with the carpenter of this ship. He is a Boston man. His name is Bentley, and we will be well entertained by him." So we dined on board the *Porcupine* on beef steaks and fine green peas. After dinner I said to Mr. Napier that my inclination was to see the camp. I said if it would be disagreeable to him I would not attempt it. He said he could not advise me to but I must take my own pleasure, so I took it upon me to undertake it. I sat out on a long sand bank, [so] near as our bank at Salem from the Channel to Long Wharf, and when I came to the first sentry I could have wish[ed] that he should

1 These were the Montmorency Falls at the mouth of the St. Charles River.

2 A pinnace was a small, light, but usually two-masted vessel normally used as a tender to larger ships.

have stopped me, but he never so much as hailed me. I still advanced to the next sentry and he never so much as hailed me, and I advanced to the top of the hill and opened the camp and saw General Wolfe at [a] distance. When I came into the camp it seemed to me like Rag Fair, for it had rained the day before, and some appeared overhauling their clothes, some going about as careless as at home, and as I advanced I saw General Wolfe a-directing a redoubt. I tarried seeing the engineer marking out the redoubt till General Wolfe was gone. I looked and saw him on an hill with his two aides-a-camps. I thought my safety depended on my pursuit to them so I stood towards them and when I approach[ed] them on the hill on the north side of Montmorency Falls an aide-a-camp said to the General, "Sir, the French are at trenching. You may see them in their shirts." General Wolfe said, "By God, there is not five thousand fighting men in all Canada," and as his custom was to carry his spyglass he took it and look[ed] at them. No sooner than he look with the glass but came a ball from the intrenchment right over our heads. General Wolfe said to me, "Sir, you are in danger!" I answered, "Sir, my curiosity for the discovery of these falls of Montmorency led me to come up to see them," and General Wolfe and his two aide-a-camp went down with him, and I followed them at a distance. And as they came towards the main guard, I keeping a look astern, I found a some this I found an order for a muster. The grand guard turned out, and what to expect I did not know, but I reflected on my seeing of General Wolfe on board the ship *Pembroke* at Halifax and to muster all my thoughts on him. So I advanced towards him and the General hailed me. "Who are you?" I answered him, "A friend!" "What department are you of?" I said of the Marine Department. "What ship?" I answered, "His Majesty's Ship *Pembroke*." "What are you on board the *Pembroke*?" My answer was "Acting Midshipman." "Where is your uniform?" I said, "I have none. I come from New England with a company of volunteers to serve His Majesty in the reduction of Canada." He said, "Do you know me?" "Yes, sir!" "Who am I?" I said, "General Wolfe, sir." "Where did you know me?" I said on board the *Pembroke* at Halifax "you came on board the *Pembroke* when you arrived at Halifax before you went on shore." And General Wolfe said, "What circumstance that you know me?" I said as I walked the quarterdeck I saw a barge rowing for our ship. I said that barge was intending for us and 4 hands was ordered for side, and "as you came on the gangway you said 'Is Captain Simcoe on board?' and immediately you crossed the quarterdeck and passed the sentry and went into the Cabin, and immediately Mr. Norman, our First Lieutenant, stepped to the gangway, and as the coxwain was coming up he said, 'Who is this Gentleman that came on board?' He said 'General Wolfe' and the orders were 'Call the Sergeant of Marines, call the Boatswain, call the Master-at-Arms!' The Sergeant of Marines ordered a file of Marines, drum and fife, six clever fellows for to man [the] side, and I expect you was in the Cabin upward of half an hour, and when you came out a ruff was beat and a-saluted you and as you crossed our quarterdeck you said 'A parcel of fine, likely men! I hope to have some good business for you!' And you went on board the *Neptune* again." And then the General asked me who commanded the *Pembroke*. I said, "John Wheelock, at present." "Sir, at present? Who did command her?" "John Simcoe, Esq." "Do you know anything about Captain Simcoe's death?" I said I did, for I took all the pains I could to inform myself of it. I said he died the 14 of May and was buried the 16. "Do you know if he made his will?" I said that the 12 [of May] the Doctor said to Mr. Norman that the Captain altered very much and that he should think it advisable to now acquaint him of his illness. So Mr. Nor[man] went into the Cabin and said to the Captain, "Sir, the Doctor think that you decline fast and would have you be apprised of it." And the next morning we bore down to the Admiral and sent our cutter on board, and Mr. Norman acquainted the Admiral that Captain Simcoe wished to have the Surgeon of the *Prince of Orange* and Lieutenant of Marines of the *Vanguard* to visit him, and the signals were made for the *Vanguard* and *Prince of Orange* to speak the Admiral. And there came on board our ship the Lieutenant of [the] *Vanguard* and [the] Doctor of [the] *Prince of Orange*, and our Captain made his will, and they returned again to their ships and we made sail [with] the whole fleet, and at 12 o'clock at night our Captain died. Then General Wolfe asked me of many more question and found that I was not an enemy to the camp. He sent a file of men with me to see me safe to the boat that I had the command of, and we all returned safe to our ship.

Note: I had command of our pinnace to row guard on the 16 of July, in the utmost danger, and Mr. Cook would have me go with him wherever he went a-sounding or discovering any remarks about the Point of Land and give me a plan of it, and he did not forget me on Banian Days[1] to dine with him.

July 31 As the preparations were made for an engagement at the proper time of the tide, Mr. Cook, at leaving our ship, said to me on our quarterdeck before he left us, "Mr. Bowen, I leave you full charge of the poop and make all the discovery you can."

Now on the 7 of September I was ordered to take command of the pinnace and to repair to the *Richmond* frigate to take further orders. All my men were ordered to obey me as their officer, and at the tides serving I was exam[ined?] by Lord Douglas and sent a forlorn hope to take up a buoy at the moor[ing] and to hail the first object I should discover and hail them three times, and if no answer to fire into them. I and my crew were acquainted with arms suitable to meet any enemy, and I discovered an object coming down to us. I said, "Bow-man, see your blunderbuss is ready and your pole-axe to cut our moorings as occasion should serve!" The object came down fast. I said to my men, "Stand by and give them a volley from your small arms as they pass us!" I hail, "Hoy!" No answer. I said, "Let fly, bow-man," and accordingly the bow-man fired and I believe every man discharged his piece at the object. Now there was a mooring with 20 buoys, one for every ship of the line. Now the next day I was told by Mr. Norman that if I had been a European I should have been prepared for my last night conduct in the alarm.

Sept. 30 This 24 hours first part blows very hard and a strong tide. Middle and latter, ditto. At 6 A.M. our signal out for a lieutenant. Ditto, our pinnace. Mr. Norman went out to answer it. He brought orders for me and all the men that came with me to get ready to board a transport, which we did. At 4 this afternoon we were all put on board a transport, which we did. At 4 this afternoon we were all put on board a cat[2] called the [*Fells*] and I went on board my brother and returned and lodge on board the cat. Note: my brother, Nathan Bowen, was master of Thomas Martin's schooner. A.M. This morning at 6 o'clock, our signal out for an officer. I went and acquainted Mr. Norman, our First Lieutenant, and he ordered our pinnace out

1 Banian Days in nautical terminology are those when no meat is served. The term derives from the dietary practices of the banyan caste in Hindu culture.

2 Cat-barks were strong, roomy vessels used as transports, storeships, and carriers.

and the Coxswain to come for his cloak, and he went on board the Admiral, and when he returned I attended at the gangway, and when he came in he said to me, "I have some good news for you sir. You and all the Marblehead men are to get ready to go on board a transport for Boston. So I infor[med] my people and they began to get ready. Note: the Purser ordered the Steward to reduce our provision from the Cook, our Captain's Clerk and the Purser settling the accounts and getting our discharges ready, which were not complete till 4 o'clock P.M. when we set off ... Captain Wheelock looked out of the quarter gallery [and] gave orders to man ship and ready to sail.

Oct. 1 Was put on board a cat the first night and the next day I was put on board an other ship with the people that come with me and from the *Pembroke*, and then came the Marblehead men from the *Squirrel* on board this ship, which is the *Thornton*, of New York, John Elkshaw commander, a ship about 500 tons. And all the Provincials were ordered on board this ship, and the Honorable Colonel Will Howe came on board and a captain and lieutenant and servants, all passengers for Boston. Note: the Marblehead men that were on board the *Squirrel*, their names are as follows:

John Melzerd	Returned	Francis Mesalt	Died
Thomas Dove	Returned	Roper Linsted	not returned
William Mathews	Ditto	William Corkering	not returned
Samuel Corferin	Ditto	Charles Jacobs	Returned
John Slateman	Ditto	William Uncals	Ditto
John Goldsmith	Died	Walter Stover	not returned
Thomas Walpy	Returned	Samuel Lines	Died
Samuel Look	Did not return	Thomas Peach	Died

Note: the whole of the Provincials that were discharged on the 30 of September were 160, and all put on board the *Thornton* well. But on the 12 of October the first died, which was Nathan Baker. We sailed from Quebec October the 8 and arrived at Boston on November the 10, and I saw 35 buried on the passage, and I have their names and the time of their death. Note: Admiral Sir Charles Saunders left the east end of Orleans the same day we left Quebec, with 3 three-deckers, viz. *Neptune*, 90, *Royal William*, 85, *Princess Amelia*, 80.

1760

I tarried on shore this winter. About the twentieth of January 1760, I petitioned the General Court, and they gave me 32.6.[1]

Note: I spent all the remainder of this year in attending our General Court petitioning for my being rated as a midshipman on board the ship *Pembroke*, and I was ranked as a Subaltern by our General Court, and I received pay accordingly. I tarried at home until May 1760. Then I entered [as] master of a transport for Canada and carried 28 head of cattle to Quebec and imployed a-wooding from Orleans to Quebec.

1762

Aug. 1 Abreast of Liscomb's Harbor.[2] At 10 A.M. came on board nine canoes with 2 or 3 Indians in each canoe. There came a breeze to the south. I a-turning out, the Frenchman came to take the helm from me, but so drunk I could not cope with him and kept the helm myself. Our decks full of Indians with muskets. I mustered up my French and told the Frenchman that I would go into Liscomb's Harbor and treat them all, as I saw three schooners go in the last evening. I was in hopes of assistance, but they seeing a brig I made them quit us and I escaped this time and got off clear. Note: I left Mr. Smethurst at Halifax to go by land to Fort Cumberland.

Aug. 2 At noon I spoke a shallop[3] direct from Newfoundland who saw a sloop which they said was a French privateer and had chase[d] three of our schooners and themselves and fired a shot at them. She was a black sides white bottom, gaff topsail. The next morning at 2 o'clock A.M., the 3 day [of August] I fell in with Su[?] a sloop laying under her foresail. I jibed mainsail and got clear of her, so when the fog was off the sloop would be chasing our schooners so I could not speak one.

This I passed till the 19 [of August] before I could get back at Bay

---

1 32 shillings and sixpence.

2 Liscomb's Harbor lies east of Halifax on the coast of Nova Scotia.

3 To speak a vessel is to stop a vessel at sea and speak to the master and/or crew.

Verte[1] by fog and no pilot put off by the sloop and the back [of] our rudder gone. So the season for Quebec passes.

Aug. 26 et seq. Sailed from the Bay Verte. Arrived at Carricutt[2] the 30 where I find a French priest and a number of Frenchmen in ambush, as all Frenchmen were called in by the English government. On the 3[1 of August] at noon came on board a large canoe with eight as stout men as are commonly seen and examined our sails, cable, ropes, and all our accommodations, speaking all in French, but I understood all they said. The priest on board the same time. After they were gone I went on shore and acquainted Mr. Smethurst and found a large collection of men and women Indians all painted. I hurried Mr. Smethurst off, and he persuaded a lad to take us out the northern wa[y?], which he did and saved the second time.

Sept. 1 et seq. The last evening we got safe out of Carricutt, and finding the season so far spent I advised Mr. Smethurst not to attempt the River St. Lawrence, for we could not expect to get down again this winter, and we went for Bay Verte again. Landed our cargo, took oysters for Halifax, where we arrived the 27 [of September]. Sold my oysters, took what freight I could get and a good pilot for Fort Cumberland, and sailed October the 9 for Fort Cumberland, where I arrived the 31 [of October] and sailed from Cumberland November 29. December the 1 at Annapolis.[3] The 10 left Annapolis. Beat and drove off as far as St. George's Bank[4] and arrived at Marblehead the 20 [of December] with eight men, neither wood, water, or pro[visions].

1763

This spring I engaged with Mr. Smethurst to carry the *Rambler* to Boston, and after I was discharge from her Mr. Smethurst recommended me to Captain George Dimon his chief mate in ship *Atlantic* at Portsmouth, owned by Mr. William Temple, and I went to

1 Bay Verte is in the Northumberland Strait on the Nova Scotia–New Brunswick border.

2 Carricut is Caraquet, on the south shore of Chaleur Bay in the Gulf of St. Lawrence.

3 Fort Cumberland and Annapolis are both in Nova Scotia: the former at the head of the Bay of Fundy, and the latter on the south shore of the Bay.

4 St. George's Bank is Georges Bank off the Massachusetts coast.

Portsmouth in a brig with Captain William Whipple [as] a passenger, and I had charge of ship *Atlantic*, and I went to the Road at the Island of Shoals and took on board 2000 quintals of pollock[1] and returned to Portsmouth again and completed all her loading and [then] left her.

July. I engaged with Jonathan Warner Esq. to go in his ship *Patty* with Captain Monsieur Bunbury as Chief Mate to the Grenards,[2] and if a freight should be had I was to carry the ship to London. And we sailed from Portsmouth the 9 and arrived at the Grenards [ ] of August. And Captain Bunbury sold [the] ship and cargo and I could not do better than to take passage with Captain [James] Gilmore on a brig [*Success*] of Mr. Warner's. Note: an English sloop of war, the *Beaver*, came to the Grenards to winter. [I] very sickly at the Grenards. Captain Bunbury at [ ] self very sick. As soon as the brig was ready we sailed.

Bowen called this "A South East view of the town of Marblehead as it appeared this 6th day of November 1763 the last time of my going to sea for 20 years." The churches, from left to right are St. Michael's; the Old Meeting House; and the New Meeting House. The vessel in the harbor is the brig, *Success*, on which Bowen had just returned from Grenada in the West Indies.

1 Pollock was before refrigeration considered a low-grade fish.

2 "Grenards" refers to Grenada in the West Indies.

1764

The first of this year I was very sick in the spring. The smallpox broke out at Boston, and when I was well enough I had the care of a watchhouse at the entr[ance] of the Town [of Marblehead], and afterwards I assisted in fixing rigging for Colonel Jeremiah Lee, brig *Africa*, a guineaman.[1] Note: My father's wife Hannah died May the 3, and he married again May the 27 to Mary Boden, widow to Ambrose Boden. Note: Hannah Reed died this year, and my daughter Hannah [was] born. I was employed the rest of the year about rigging. I lived in a house of my father's, and I fitted it up and it was sold.

1765

This spring my stepmother would have my father to sell this house to Mr. John Fowler and I to remove to a chamber in a house of his called Norden's House, and I did so about May. I have as much employ about rigging as I could wish under the unhappy circumstances I am under, for I have no loft that I can hire and [am] forced to fix sails at the halfs and take goods for my pay, but I do not know how to do better.

1766

This year I have as much business at rigging on shore as I could do under the unhappy burden of not having a rigging loft, for as our customs was for the sailmakers to find a rigging loft for all their customers I was obliged, when I had any suit of rigging to fix, I was oblige to shift my tackle and gear to the sailmaker's loft that should make their sails, and when I should have employ to fix sail[s] I was oblige to allow the sailmaker one-half for loft rent.

---

1 A guineaman was a vessel trading to the coast of Guinea; hence, a slave-ship.

A memorandum of what I have done at rigging since the year 1766 commenced—[1]

February	8	Schooner *Dolly* to 4 single shrouds @ 3/1 2 jibstay 3 straps	0 -16- 0
Ditto	17	Thomas Proctor to fixing one half at 3	1 -10-
Ditto	26	fixed a jibstay for Captain Jonathan Glover	0 - 3 - 0
March	10	fixed a pair of shrouds for Joseph Pedrick	0 - 6 - 0
Ditto	22	fixed two pair of shrouds for Captain Griste	0 -13 - 4
May	22	John Prince to fixing a sloop's rigging	3 - 0 - 0
June	19	Michael Bowden to fixing a schooner's rigging	3 - 0 - 8
Ditto	28	Joseph Howard to fixing a small schooner's rigging	2 - 0 - 0
August	2	Delivered the brig *St. Paul*'s rigging to Colonel Lee[?]	11 - 6 - 8
Ditto	6	Colonel [Jeremiah] Lee to fixing schooner *Eagle* rigging	3 - 0 - 0
Ditto	22	Colonel Lee to fixing a sloop for John Patton	3 - 0 - 0
September	18	Colonel Lee to fixing schooner *Swan* rigging	3 - 0 - 0
November	11	Captain Israel Foster to fixing a schooner's rigging	3 - 0 - 0
December	11	Captain Thomas Gerry to fixing schooner rigging	3 - 0 - 0
Ditto	24	to half Captain Griste's	1 -10-
Captain Knott Martin overhaul his rigging			2 - 0 -
Sloop *Swallow* to 2 main sheets stri[...]			0 - 3 -
			£40 -02- 0

[1] The figures in these columns are in pounds, shillings, and pence, in Massachusetts Lawful Money. The price of "4/8" reads "four shillings, eight pence."

Tarring parceling	5 - 0 -
My wife making colors[1]	
Richard Skinner his ensign 4/8 J. Prince per 6/8	£5 -11 - 4
Mr. Bowde[n] an ensign 4/8 Gage ensign 4/4 A f[...] ensign 68 9 3/4	0 -18 - 8
To brig *St. Paul* a sail 15 Schooner *Swan* and *Eag[le]* 8/4	1 - 3 - 4
Captain Ballister suit 12 Comm ensign 4 Jack 12	1 - 4 - 0
Gordon Jack 3/4 Forster Jack 2/5	0 - 5 - 9
Howard's Jack 1 1/4	0 - 1 - 4
	4 - 4 - 5

1767

I am the chief rigger in Marblehead, but under so great a disadvantage darst not engage a suit of rigging without asking who makes the sails, for our merchants will not let me have a loft to myself as long as they can get jobbers to fix their rigging free of loft rent, and between jobbing at rigging and my wife's making color[s] we touch and go. Poor times with us.

1768

By the goodness of God I have received a great many favors from Colonel Jeremiah Lee, Esq., who gives me all the benefit of all his transients' rigging as well as his own and making of all his colors [and] stranger. So I think I am much favor[ed] by him, and as we have so good a ropewalk now in Marblehead I hope to have a loft to myself, as I could wish to have some benefit.

1 Colors, ensigns, and jacks were all flags. "My wife making colors" is a heading for what follows.

1769

This year I was well employed. As soon as Eastern men was supplied by Colonel Lee and Mr. Robert Hooper, Esq., I made both ends meet very well, although much sickness in my family.

1770

This year plenty of work at rigging, as I expect that our ropewalk bears the best character in this Province. Colonel Lee and Mr. Hooper imports the best of hemp from Europe and supplies as cheap and on as reasonable terms as anybody.

1778

This is a year of trouble to me. I was drafted twice as a soldier and taken by Nathan Brown and carried before old [Josiah] Ward the 25 of March and worried along the summer, sometimes a-wooding. That fall then they trained with me so much that they would have me to get bondsmen for me not to speak nor look nor deny them of my money when draft[ed]. So I could not get bondsmen. It was determined to send me on board the Guard Ship at Boston, but meeting with Captain Thomas Boyles he took me his Mate out of their way. Note: a French fleet lay at Nantasket of 13 line [...] ships.

Appendix A: Ashley Bowen, "Courtship of Dorothy Chadwick"

[This passage comes from a separate manuscript known as "The Courtship of Dorothy Chadwick (1757–1761)" at the Marblehead Historical Society. It was published in Smith, ed., *Journals of Ashley Bowen*, 1: 47–51, and is reproduced here in its entirety. The last paragraph contains a good summary of Bowen's service in the Seven Years War.]

About the first of September as our carpenters began to rip up our sloop [*Olive*] they found every beam end in her rotten, and days growing shorter, I had a time of it, for she proved so rotten that she had every beam and knee new and 18 top timber on one side and 17 on the other, and, as she was employed in carrying horses, she had a very short quarterdeck and all her stern timbers [were] rotten. I advised with Mr. Hooper to run our main deck quite aft to her sternpost and to continue our quarterdeck 8 feet further forward in order to strengthen her. So our main deck run fore and aft [made of] 3-inch pine plank, and we had to new sheath her 3 strake, and we did not finish her at Salem till November. And after we came to Marblehead we took on board lumber to [make] hogshead with in our hold and then I took on board one tier of hogs[heads] fish and mas[?] with a deckload of lumber. And I sailed from Marblehead for St. Eustatius November the 28. I arrived at St. Eustatius on December the 25 and I delivered my cargo to Mr. James Freeman and our sloop cost so much to repair her, and having a good opportunity to get home, and [I] left Mr. James Freeman's employ and came home to Marblehead with my B[rother Nathan] Bowen.

Now, as concerning marriage. In 1749 I boarded with Mr. Elias Currel when I was Mate of brig *Duke of Cumberland*, and his daughter expected me to pay suit to her but as I shifted my board to Mr. Simpson Boden's, I became acquainted with one Mary Andros, and I paid a great attention to her. And as young women do sometimes try [their] progress so they tried me and put under my head a plate, knife, and fork with a blade bone of lamb tied up in a napkin. And I dreamed I saw an elderly woman with a girl of about 10 years old a-standing by her side, and I thought that the girl was the one I was to have. So, when I discovered the plot, I could not fix my affection on Molly as I did before time, for of all the women I ever saw I could not ever fancy one to wife till I saw her, which was about one hundred leagues at sea on my passage home from the West Indies in sloop *Olive*. The first of June 1757 in the afternoon as I lay down about 3 P.M., I saw a woman sitting on my [sea] chest. I expected I was awake, and I examined her face and saw five moles on her right cheek, and some other remark.

I arrived at Marblehead in June 1757, and when I came on shore I went to my lodgings to Mrs. Mary Boden's. There I found two or three likely young women [for] as Mrs. Boden was a tailoress she had many girls to learn the trade. One Dorothy Chadwick, a young woman from Boxford, served the last summer with Mrs. Boden and came down to Marblehead to finish her service, and I sailed the morning before, mate of Captain Philip Lewis, in December, and I was taken by the French and afterwards I had the command of sloop *Olive* owned by Mr. James Freeman. I examined two of the former young women and found no moles nor marks. After I had delivered my cargo and laid up my sloop and cloth[ed] myself, I determined to go out in the country to see my sister, Sarah Johnson, widow to Mr. Ebenezer Johnson, and I agreed with Mrs. Cowell for her horse to go off tomorrow, Saterday. Note: Mr. Benjamin Russell boarded with me, and we lodged together in one bed, and the evening before I was to set off Mr. Russell asked me if I was bound to Andover.[1] I said I was. He said he would send a letter to Dolly's sister, and he saith she was a fine young woman. Note: Mr. Russell had courted Dolly all winter and had carried her up to Boxford, and by all reports was espoused to her but not married. So, I said to Mr. Russell, "If you will write a letter to Mrs. Mehitable Chadwick I will carry it or the one to Dorothy." He said I might write one and he would sign it. So I wrote a letter in Mr. Russell's name and gave myself as good a character as we thought was my true one, and when Mr. Russell came home to breakfast I shew him the letter to read. [He said] "I do not want to read it, but I will sign it." I sealed it up and set off for Andover. [I] came to my sister Johnson's and after dinner we went to Mr. Stephen Barker's, and there I saw Mrs. Mehitable Chadwick, and I gave her Mr. Russell's letter and she opened it, and as she read I a-looking at her but could not find any moles or mark.

So, after Mehitable Chadwick had read Mr. B. Russell letter and I well examined her face, I thought to pay her a visit. I went to Andover Meeting

1 Boxford and Andover were adjoining farming villages in Massachusetts, inland from Marblehead.

House on Sunday. In the evening I went to Mr. Stephen Barker's and tarried with M. Chadwick till midnight, but I thought it but lost labor to think of ever coming so far as Andover for a wife. She put me to bed in order to wait another night, as Sunday night did not so well suit her. In the morning after a fine breakfast, I had my horse brought to the gate. Mehitable and I stood a-talking the affair over. I asked her if it was much out of my way to go and see Dolly. She might wish to send some word to Mr. Russell. She directed me the road as exact as if she had given me a plan, and, coming to a shoemaker's shop, I went and inquired of the master of the shop if one Dorothy Chadwick was in the house. He conducted me into his house where I saw two nice looking young women, but I could find no moles nor marks. Soon after, came in the very person I expected I saw come on board the sloop *Olive* when I was, I expect, one hundred leagues to sea. As soon as I saw her I do not know how to express my feeling unless it was as when Mary salut[ed] Elizabeth [and] the Babe leaped in her womb for joy. So, they all quitted the room and I had a fair opportunity to examine her real moles and marks with real sweet kisses of real substance of lips and breast and all the qualifications a young woman could be endowed with to make a man happy. After my expressing to how I felt when I went to sea that morning—"had I tarried till you came to Marblehead I expects that as we should have had an opportunity of being acquainted with one another—for if I had seen you before Mr. Russell you would have given me so much satisfaction that I expect that we should have been marry. But now, as it is, will you keep my company for the future? I will pay all the attention in my power to you, and if you will receive my suit and acquaint me where I shall find you I will wait on you the next Thursday even[ing]," which answer was, "Be patient."

I expect I tarried with Dolly at Mr. David Chadwick nearly an hour and then sat off for home, and I inquired of Mrs. Boden and she said that Mr. Russell sent her up to Boxford on purpose to see Dolly and to find whether she thought that Dolly had regard enough for him as to marry him, and she saith that she was sure that Dolly had not regards enough for to marry him, notwithstanding that he had left earrings and rings that were his mother's and she had shirts to make for him. Then I said that she was [to be] my wife. Then I came to Salem and I saw Mr. Benjamin Porter of Boxford, and I wrote a letter and I sent it by him to his son, Moses Porter, for Dolly Chadwick, and on Thursday I hired a horse at Salem and went to Boxford and saw Dolly and never parted her company till married, and we had six living children.

Married in May 1758. Our first child, a son, born in January 1759, named Ashley, and died August 1760. Our [second] son Ashley was born February 2, 1761. February 11, 1764, our daughter Hannah was born. March 24, 1766 was born a daughter, her name is Dorothy. July the 10 [1766] our daughter Dorothy died. September the 30, 1767 our son Nathan born. January the 8, 1770 our son Ambrose born. Our son Ambrose died May the 31, 1770. My wife Dorothy died on August 17, 1771. I married Mary Shaw December the 8, 1771. My daughter Mary born December the 1, 1774. My daughter Sally Ashley born May the 12, 1776. On Monday, June the 25, 1781 died my wife Mary, and I married Mrs. Hannah Graves, widow to Mr. Jacob Graves, formerly of Lynn, and I had six children by her. Married in February 1782 and had two children born in October 1782, a son and a daughter—the son named Edward Ashley; the daughter Martha Galusha—christened by Mr. Nathan Fisher of Salem, September the 28, 1783. And my daughter Elizabeth was born March the 8, 1785 and my son Ambrose was born May the 11, 1788 and was christened by Mr. Thomas Fitch Oliver, and on Sunday ninety one a son was born whose name was Daniel, born August the 7, 1791. November the 16, 1795 died our son Daniel. On November the 26, 1798 our son Ambrose died, aged ten years and 5 month and 25 day, and on Thursday, March the 30, 1797 our present son Daniel was born [and] christened by Mr. William Harris at St. Michael's. My son Nathan died at Dominica in W[est] I[ndies] in March the 27, 1793 [1794], mate of Captain Ebenezer Graves, aged 26 years, 5 months and 26 days. My daughter Mary died November the 28, 1796.

Now I must turn to my travels again. And so, after my arriving in sloop *Olive*, [I] thought that Mr. Freeman was a good deal dissatisfied and came on board with a merchant in order [to] sell the sloop, and as I had a fine opportunity to get home with my brother Nathan, then master of a brig of Colonel Jeremiah Lee's, Esquire, I left the sloop *Olive* and came home to seek bread. And the first thing that I did I took a wife and shipped myself Mate of Captain Mr. [Michael] Coombs and went with him to Lisbon and did tolerably well. After we returned I went to housekeeping and I went one trip a-wooding and then tarried at home all winter.

We three brothers had each a vessel in 1758, and in the spring of 1759 we neither of us had a vessel. So our General Court appointed us 3 and Mr. William Pousland and Mr. Thomas Nichols, both mates of Mr.

Hooper's ships, but none of them would accept the offer but myself, and I enlisted and I got 17 [volunteers] that day, and I got myself ready and I sailed for Halifax the 12 of April 1759 with 32 seamen besides myself and arrived at Halifax the 16 and all [were ordered] on board our ships. Sixteen and myself on board the *Pembroke* of 60 guns and 16 on board the *Squirrel* of 20 guns. So we went to Quebec. Discharged at Quebec September the 30 and came home in a transport ship [of] 500 tons and arrived at Boston the 10 November, and I came home to Marblehead. I found my wife and son quite well and all my father's family well, and I tarried at home all winter a-petitioning our General Court for extraordinary pay for my extraordinary service. And in May 1760 I engaged with Mr. Joseph Weare of old York to go in his schooner *Swallow* [as] master and pilot for the river St. Lawrence. So I sailed from Boston May the 25, 1760 with 28 head of cattle and arrived at Quebec June 28. The 30 we landed our cattle at the Island of Orleans safe, and we spent the summer a-wooding from Island Orleans to Quebec, and in the fall we went to Mount Royal and lay all winter at the River Sorel[1] till April the 20, 1761 [when we] came through Lake St. Peters and to Quebec. Arrived at Boston May 27, 1761. I arrived from Quebec May the 27, 1761. I tarried at home about rigging all summer and at home all winter.

---

1 Mount Royal was Montreal. Sorel is on the St. Lawrence River halfway between Montreal and Quebec.

Appendix B: Ashley Bowen, Journal Entries Relating to the Seven Years War and the Expedition Against Quebec, 1759

[Unlike the Autobiography, which Bowen wrote many years after the Quebec expedition, the materials in this section are contemporary to the events described. The material was drawn from the daily entries in Ashley Bowen, "Journal of the Siege of Quebec, et seq. (1759–1761)" at the Marblehead Historical Society and published originally in Smith, ed., *Journals of Ashley Bowen*, 44: 57–97. What follows consists of excerpts from the Smith edition. All are in Bowen's hand, except the entry of July 15, 1759, which was written for him.]

1. Voyage to Quebec

Apr. 16 This 24 hours first part foggy. At 5 P.M. I saw Ashmetoggin bearing NW, distance 4 leagues. At sunset I saw Cape Sambro.[1] Middle, clear and cold, little wind or calm. At 5 this morning we found ourself in the chops of Halifax and the wind right ahead. At 8 ditto. Captain Goreham with another gentleman went on shore in a barge we brought down. At noon we anchored at Halifax. At 3 this afternoon I went on shore and waited on the Admiral, and he gave me a very kind reception and desired me to wait on him on the morrow, and I lodged on board the schooner *Apollo* and [also] all my people. All is well.

Apr. 17 This morning at nine I, with my people, went on shore and waited on Admiral Durell. He sent us all on board his ship, and then the Admiral sent sixteen of us on board the *Pembroke* and sixteen on board the *Squirrel*. This day I wrote a small line to my wife.

* * * * *

May 1 Ditto weather. P.M. anchored here Vice Admiral [Charles] Saunders with seven sail of the line, viz.:

---

1 Cape Sambro is in Nova Scotia, just west of Halifax.

Neptune of 90 guns, 750 men
Royal William of 84 guns, 720 men
Dublin
Orford
Shrewsbury
Medway
and *Stirling Castle*

Likewise a fire ship and some transports. Ditto, Admiral Durell saluted Admiral Saunders with 15 guns as Admiral Saunders returned with 15 ditto and the ship with three cheers. Saunders returned one ditto. [The] garrison saluted Admiral Saunders with 13 guns. Ditto, Admiral Saunders made signal of his Division to moor. Ditto [a signal] for all lieutenants. Ditto Admirals Saunders and Durell saluted General [James] Wolfe's going ashore. Ditto the garrison returned the salute. A.M. the longboat employ[ed] in carrying pickets on board transports. We have the Article of War read on board and the new Act.

★ ★ ★ ★ ★

May 5 This 24 hours first and middle foggy with rain. Latter, moderate and clear. At ½ past 10 down topgallant yards. At 4 A.M. up topgallant yards. At 7 ditto Admiral made signal to weigh. Ditto weighed and came to sail with Rear Admiral Durell in His Majesty's Ship *Princess Amelia, Vanguard, Devonshire, Captain, Centurion, Prince* [*of*] *Orange*, and *Pembroke, Richmond* and *Squirrel* frigates, *Boscawen* tender, and three transports. The whole fleet consists of 13 sail.

2. Quebec Campaign

May 28 This 24 hours first part cloudy, a fresh gale. At 5 P.M. came to at the island of Coudre with all our fleet except the *Prince of Orange* and her prize. As we came to we broke our best bower about 2½ feet from the stock. Let go our small bower, hove up our stock of best bower and moored with our sheet anchor to the eastward.[1] At 5 A.M. Admiral made a signal to land the troops, and we all landed our troops on the island of Coudre.[2]

1 The small bower and best bower are two bow anchors of different sizes. The sheet anchor is the largest of a ship's anchors, used mainly in emergencies.

2 Coudre is an island about 50 miles downstream from Quebec.

May 29 This 24 hours first part moderate with some rain. At 8 P.M. embarked all the troops. Found no French on shore [but] plenty of horses, some calves, hogs, &c.

May 30 This 24 hours first part moderate with rain. At 7 P.M. received on board a sheet anchor from on board the *Vanguard*. Bent sheet cable. Middle and latter, fresh gales. Down topgallant yards.

May 31 This 24 hours first part fresh gale. Middle and latter, ditto. Our small beer is done. Served wine, a short pint a man. Very strong tides runs here.

★ ★ ★ ★ ★

July 15 First part moderate and hazy with lightning all round. Remainder moderate and cloudy. At 3 P.M. our signal out for an officer. At 9 our batteries to the SW of Point Levy began to bombard Quebec. At midnight we [had] a very smart engagement on the North Shore all round Falls of Montmorency of great guns, small arms, howitzers, and bombshells which lasted 3 hours. At 6 sent our longboat and pinnace with an officer to land artillery. Ditto, our signal out for an officer. At 10 A.M. anchored here the *Vesuvius* fireship from the Isle Coudre.

3. Battle of the Plains of Abraham and the Capture of Quebec

Sept. 13 First part at 6 P.M. Admiral made a signal for all boats manned and armed, and we went and made a feint at the River St. Charles, and at 11 I repaired on board our ship *Pembroke*. This 24 hours first, middle, and latter parts clear weather. At 2 A.M. a smart firing to the S-west of us. At 5 ditto, General Wolfe landed about 3 miles above the town. He immediately took the first post. At 8 General Wolfe engaged the enemy and fell in the field of battle. General Montcalm dropped at the same time with Wolfe. FINIS.[1]

Sept. 14 This 24 hours first part moderate. At 4 P.M. Admiral made [a] signal for all boats manned and armed and 19 men and an officer to go above the town. At 8 the boats made a feint on [St.] Charles River. A.M. Loosed sail to dry.

Sept. 15 This 24 [hours] first part moderate and clear. P.M. hand[ed] sails. Middle, cloudy. Latter, much wind and rain. We received 20 long-boats alongside and moored them astern till flood [tide]. At 12 night all

---

1 Battle of the Plains of Abraham.

the boats set off as did our own longboat with a Master's Mate. Anchored here His Majesty Ship *Northumberland* from the Isle Madame.

Sept. 16 This 24 hours first, middle, and latter parts clear. Our batteries continued firing off shot and shells. At 6 A.M. sent for fresh beef.

Sept. 17 Ditto weather. At 2 P.M. sailed His Majesty Ship *Captain*. Admiral Saunders made a signal for all lieutenants, and we cleared ship in order to go against the town of Quebec. At 10 o'clock A.M. Admiral made a signal to unmoor. Ditto, unmoored, as did his ship and the other nine sail of the line. At[?] 11 sail of the line and the *Richmond* frigate. At 11 anchored all the fleet and moored about a mile and a half below Quebec. Our batteries firing as before.

Sept. 18 This 24 hours first part close weather. P.M. our batteries all ceased firing. Middle and latter, much wind and rain. At 7 A.M. our shipping hoisted their colors and the enemy hoisted two flags of truce, one on the barbet battery and the other on the Citadel. Some boats came past the town.

Sept. 19 This 24 hours first, middle, and latter parts clear. At 3 P.M. we had the happiness of seeing Eng[lish] colors marched into the City of Quebec and our troops soon struck their flags of truce. At 6 our barge went with a Master's Mate to take possession of the lower town. Most of the ships sent a boat to the lower town. This evening came down all the boats that was above the town. A.M. our signal out for an officer. At 9 Admiral made a signal to unmoor. Cleared hawse, did not unmoor. The *Orford*'s people and boats went on board their ship.

Appendix C: Smallpox

1. Ashley Bowen, "A Memorandum of the Smallpox from the First Discovery at Marblehead, 1773"

[This account of the outbreak of the Smallpox epidemic in Marblehead, 1773–74, comes from his "Memorandum of the Smallpox Epidemic (1773–1774)," owned by the Marblehead Historical Society and published in Smith, ed., *Journals of Ashley Bowen*, 45: 344–45.]

About the first of June, Captain John Wooldredge in his schooner returned from a cruise on the Banks. It happened that while out that Mr. Wooldredge and Mr. William Mathews, one of the crew, went on board a French ship, as tis common for our fishermen to do and that Mathews brought with him a piece of Castile soap, and he saith nothing else from the French. But the day fortnight after Mathews's wife had washed his sea-clothes she broke out and swelled to a great degree. Doctor Joseph Lines was sent for, and all hands said Mrs. Mathews was poisoned, and Mary Ingalls attended said Mathews while sick.

It is to be understood that this Mrs. Sarah Mathews was daughter to Mrs. Sarah Shaw, widow, sister to Mr. Ebenezer Stacey, deceased, and I married James Shaw's widow, [he being a] son [-in-law] to said Sarah Shaw and that Mary Ingalls was [another] daughter to Mrs. Shaw.

About the 20 of June 1773 my wife went to see Sarah Mathews, and her sister came here to see her, and I sent for wife directly. And when she returned she told me that Mrs. Mathews was so much poisoned that her head was like to bust open. I asked what they did for her. She told me that Mol Ingalls did wash her with salt water and the liquor of elder and that Joseph Lines attend[ed] her. It happened about this time a girl, daughter to Mr. Isaac Williams, was broke out with poison to a very great degree and got well of it.

As this Sarah Mathews had a daughter named Sarah Hindley, and of course assisted in nursing her mother, catched the said poison, and [so] Mol Ingalls [and] some of the neighbors washed her with salt water and liquor of elder as all the neighbors all round took their turns to watching as in any other sickness. And on Thursday, July 15, 1773 my wife went to see her relative, and when she returned told me that Sarah Hindley was full as bad poisoned as her mother had been before and further said that if she had been acquainted with smallpox she would be sure that they had it.

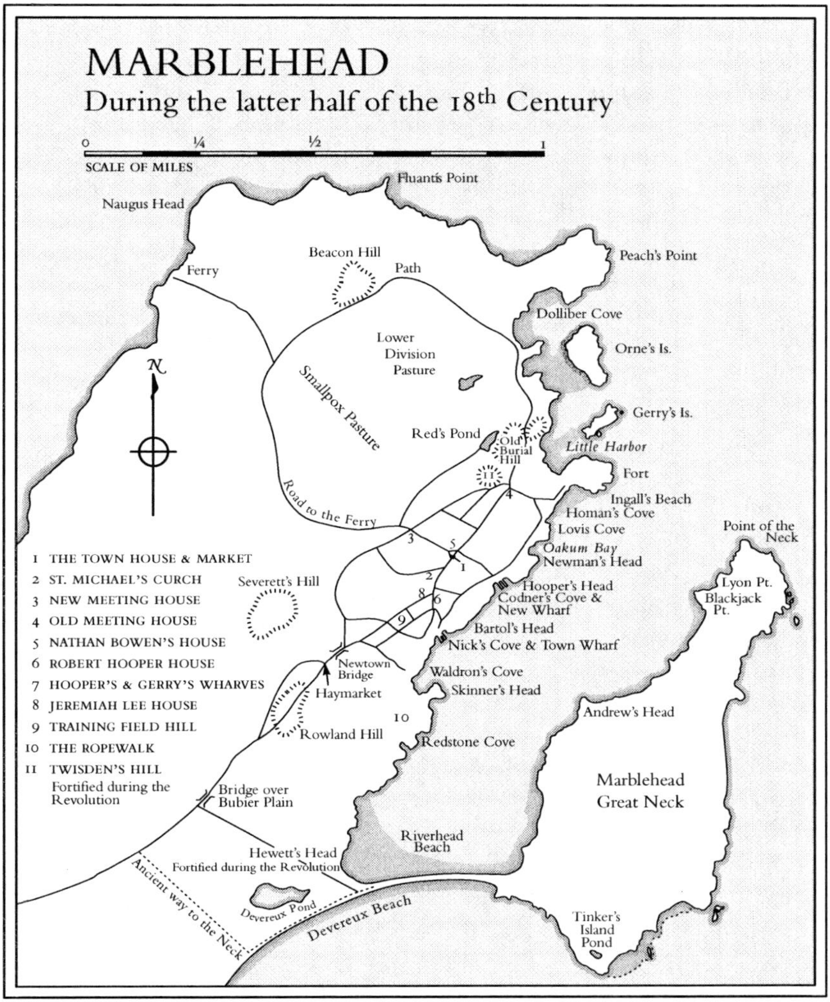

However, all matters were overlook[ed], viz. respect[ing] of their having the smallpox, although John Melzard swore to it that it was the smallpox [...] and about the 20 of July Mother Shaw was taken herself and Mol Ingalls spared no pains for to get assistance to her mother, and tis supposed that nearly an hundred or more of Mother Shaw's relations and friends frequented the house all the time from her first complaint. Mol would have it that her mother was struck with old age, she being 79 year. My wife was sent for to see her mother before she died.

On Thursday, July 22, 1773, this morning my wife went to see her Mother Shaw before breakfast. I coming home, she told me that her mother was a-dying with old age. I being very busy at my loft give no great attention; however, this evening I came home [and] I found my wife abed. I inquired the reason [and] found her to be ill of a fever. My sisters came and pound[1] up her head and made her some tea of balm. I sat up with her the fore part of the night. Latter part, she seemed somewhat better.

[On July 23] her sister came to attend her whom had had the smallpox and tarried till the evening. Then she returned home. I sent for a watcher, but the next news it was said to be the smallpox and that five or six was complaining of it at Mother Shaw's, so could get nobody to watch.

This morning I was satisfied that my wife had the smallpox and her sister came again. This afternoon I removed her to her Mother Shaw's. At 9 o'clock in morning I went and acquainted the Selectmen and the whole town was in an uproar about smallpox, and I went and saw Sarah Mathews and her daughter who had both had the smallpox.[2] There was a fence directed both ways [across] the road, and at 3 o'clock afternoon I removed my wife to her Mother Shaw's where she taught the pox for some of them to attend her, but Mol [Ingalls] was very hard to be persuaded that it was the smallpox although so many was ill with it.

2. Ashley Bowen, Journal Entries on the Smallpox Epidemic and Inoculation Controversy (1773–74)

[Bowen's description of the inoculation controversy displays a skeptical, even satiric, tone, couching his rendition of events in a quasi-military metaphor, which should be compared to the more sympathetic version presented in the *Essex Gazette* (Appendix C3). This material comes from Bowen's "Day Book (1766–1775)," owned by the Marblehead Historical Society and his "Interleaved Almanacs (1773–1775)," owned by the James Duncan Phillips Library of the Peabody-Essex Museum, both published in Smith, ed., *Journals of Ashley Bowen*, 45: 351–53, 361–62, 366–67, 382–83, 386–87.]

---

1 Pound has an archaic meaning: wrapped up.

2 Selectmen were elected town officials.

July 22 This day employed on straps for sloop, Galley and Rich, and schooner, Sproul.[1] Delivered a boom pennant to Colonel Lee, schooner *Abigail*. Employed John Rimshire half day. Sailed [schooner *Sally*], Alexander Ross, for Europe [Bilbao].

July 23 This day employed on schooner, Sproul, shrouds. Delivered a burgee and Jack and ensign mended to schooner *Darby* and [a] vane. Served two ties to for schooner *Darby*. Wife quite ill. [Delivered] boom pennant to Captain Lewis, schooner *William*. Employed Dennin and John Rimshire a day each.

July 24 Employed on schooner, Sproul's shroud. This day I have the misfortune to find my wife to have the smallpox. Mrs. Mary Bowen removed. Sarah Gould, Sarah Reith Rogers, Ann Rogers widow, Mercy [or Mary] Brinto [?], Mrs. Chambers, [and] Mrs. Dodd all have taken smallpox at the same time and many more are much suspected to have it. Delivered Captain Pote fore-topmast rigging to himself. Employed Dennin [and] Rimshire a day.

This day [July 25] I attended the fence at Captain William Courtis's warehouse. Note: the women that were now complaining are Mrs. Sarah Gould, wife of Mr. Thomas Gould; Sarah Reith [Rogers]; widow Ann Rogers; Mrs. Clark, widow; Mercy [or Mary] Brette [?]; Mrs. Chambers; and Mary Dodd, wife of Mr. Thomas Dodd; and Elisha Rogers are all supposed to have taken the smallpox at one time. Many more are suspected. Note: Mr. Thomas Gould supposed he hath the smallpox before [so] attended the house withinside the fence. And Mr. Thomas Dodd was so indifferent about the matter that he stayed and attended with Gould. Mother Shaw quite ill.

* * * * *

July 28 This day smallpox day. At 5 o'clock this morning departed this life Mother Shaw with the smallPOX and was buried this forenoon over to the Neck just above Blackjack's Cove and in that plain. Some people moved to Ferry.[2] Deliver ensign and burgee to schooner *Manchester*.

* * * * *

1 Here and elsewhere, Bowen sometimes identified vessels by their masters' names. Hence, they are not italicized.

2 The Ferry refers to a neighborhood on the west side of town near the Salem ferry, where the epidemic first broke out and to which infected people were moved so as to be isolated from the rest of the town.

Oct. 14 No rigging in hand. Nobody broke out with smallpox. Great preparation of the hospital on Cat Island[1] for inoculation.

Oct. 15 The last evening Mrs. Reddan was moved to Ferry. This day no rigging in hand. This afternoon I went to Ferry to see about my things. Sandy Green's widow buried. Sailed John Hooper [in the schooner *Lynn*] for West Indies and Burnham [in the schooner *Eleanor* for West Indies]. This day came to town General Hall Jackson, Grand Physician,[2] for inoculation on Cat Island with a number of volunteers with him.

Oct. 16 This day no rigging in hand. This afternoon I went to Ferry and brought my things, viz. feathers from a bed, 1 sheet, 1 blanket, 1 bolster lift, 1 sheet, son's shirt, [...]. Great preparation for the hospital on Cat Island.

Oct. 17 This day fair and pleasant weather. Doctor H[all] Jackson at Church with a number of volunteers for inoculation. Self at Church all day, wife half.

Monday, Oct. 18 This day do nothing. Moderate. We hear of the pox breaking out at Ipswich Harbor. This day the whole that is doing is about inoculations. It seems that the first cow that they had on the isle was so discontented that she took her calf on her back and swam for the Neck and was discovered and carried back.

Oct. 19 This day all our inoculators sat off for Cat Island. Forepart much rain. Latter, fair wind NW. Moved to Ferry a child of Mrs. Uncle's. This day at noon Colonel Orne with a body of volunteers and a number of invalids landed at Cape Pus on the NW end of the Isle of Cat and laid siege to the Castle of Pox, General Jackson, commander-in-chief; General Randall, leftenant general of Castle Pox; Arnold Martin Esq., chief admiral of the white, in sloop *Ashley*. Tis supposed this siege will last thirty days. By an express from Castle Pox General Jackson had a smart engagement and wounded nearly a 100 of Colonel Orne's body of volunteers the first evening they landed, of both sexes from the age of 3 years to 60 first day, and that General Randall engaged the Colonel himself.[3]

* * * * *

Monday, Nov. 1 This day do nothing at loft. Fine weather. Wind at SW. This day at 9 o'clock A.M. the *Mercury* cruiser set off from the brig *St.*

---

1 Cat Island lies about a half-mile off Marblehead Neck.

2 Hall Jackson was a physician from Portsmouth, who had trained in England and was a proponent of inoculation.

3 Bowen's treatment of events, describing them as a pitched battle, began here to assume a more sarcastic tone.

CAT ISLAND, as seen from the entrance to Marblehead Harbour, 1773.
The large building in the center was the Inoculation Hospital; the small building to the left was the "Shifting House" where incoming and departing patients changed clothing to prevent infected garment from returning to the mainland.
The vessel on the extreme left was the hospital's cruiser, *Mercury*.

Paul for the Isle of Cat, in whom went passenger the old Nick and sundry other passenger for the Isle of Cat, with oysters and other stores for Castle Pox. At ½ past 1 P.M., the *Mercury* returned with all her passenger and returned Squire Dalton and Mr. Joseph Hooper from the Isle of Cat. Tis supposed by some that the volunteer will bring more scars than they were aware of before. The *Mercury* doth not return to the Island this afternoon. Died a child [at] Ferry.

Nov. 2 This day no rigging in hand. Arrived Captain David Lee [in the brig *Young Phoenix*] from Gibraltar with his mainmast sprung. This day I received 1½ cord of wood from Calley and Rich. This day at 11 A.M. sailed the *Mercury*, Commodore Vickery, for the Isle of Cat, in whom went passenger Mrs. Swett Hooper, Dennis and Halleys. At 1 o'clock P.M. the *Mercury* return from the Isle of Cat with the said passengers as before and Mr. Sam Giles with them who informs us that all the inhabitants at Castle Pox were well and that G[eneral] Putnam (liked Colonel Orne's daughter) so well that he took (her nature) upon him. It being the second time inoculation tis hinted that some of the b[uc]k volunteers are much more nice than wise on the willing ardor. Some are so polite as to drink nothing but Madeira abroad that can hardly get cider at home.

Nov. 3 This day received a quintal merchantable fish from Colonel Lee, Joseph Davis, and received topgallant gear from Colonel Lee, snow *Guardoqui*. This day at 10 o'clock A.M. the *Mercury* cruiser, Commodore Vickery, set off for the Isle of Cat, in whom went passenger Mr. Joseph Hooper and Mr. S. White and Mrs. Prentiss and Mrs. Harris, and a strange gentleman, Mr. E[lbridge] Gerry.[1] At one o'clock P.M. the *Mercury* returned with her said passengers. At 3 ditto the *Mercury* set [off] for the Isle of Cat with two Salem gentlemen. At dark the boat returned. Tis said there be great to be done at Castle Pox on the 5 instant. Note: Mr. Elbridge Gerry stayed at the Isle of Cat.

Nov. 4 This day I served snow *Guardoqui* topgallant gear. This day at 10 A.M. the *Mercury* cruiser set off for the Isle of Cat with provisions and sundry of Castle Pox, and the *Mercury* returned at ½ past noon. At ½ past 2 o'clock P.M. the *Mercury* sat off for the Isle of Cat, in whom went passengers William and David Lee, Esq., Nick and Finch Gordon Esq., Captain John Prince, and two of the ship crew. At ¼ after 4 ditto the *Mercury* returned with her said passengers. We hear that the Salemites are a-building an hospital for them in what they call the Great Pasture and have as many men as can work at building it.[2]

Nov. 5 This day great to do at Cat Island. This evening the Essex Hospital was illuminated and [...].[3] This morning much rain. At noon we heard the Castle guns fired and at 1 o'clock P.M. the shipping at Boston fired. At 3 P.M. the *Mercury* cruiser put off for the Isle of Cat with tar barrel and sundries for a bonfire on the Isle of Cat this evening. The inhabitants on the Isle of Cat illuminated Castle Pox and made a bonfire on the body of the Isle of Cat. The inhabitants of this town made a stage with the Pope, the Devil, and so forth and hauled it about town, and a number of our gentlemen assembled at the Royal Exchange and spent the evening and they throw eighteen sky rockets off the balcony over the town.[4] Note: the *Mercury* left Mr. Sam Giles at the Isle of Cat.

---

1 Gerry was a wealthy merchant, a proprietor of the hospital, and a prominent patriot. Later in life he served as Governor of Massachusetts and Vice-President of the United States.

2 The neighboring town of Salem constructed a similar hospital during this epidemic, which inoculated patients for close to a year and then closed in a swirl of scandal. See Gerard H. Clarfield, "Salem's Great Inoculation Controversy, 1773–1774," *Essex Institute Historical Collections*, 72 (1970), 277–96.

3 The Marblehead hospital was named the Essex Hospital after the county in which the town sat.

4 This describes Pope's Day (in England, Guy Fawkes Day), commemorating the failed attempt by English Catholics to blow up the Houses of Parliament in 1605.

* * * * *

Jan. 19, 1774 This day employed on schooner *Manchester* rigging. Delivered all her main shrouds to the master. Employed Colman 3 hours. This day I arrived at the 46 year of my age. This evening John Granday J[?] Broughton, James Delap, J. Clark, and a servant of Granday's all went to Cat Island to steal clothes that was left out a-cleaning, and they were detected by Colonel Orne, Major Pedrick, Knott Martin, Jr., Captain [Peter] Green and were delivered to the inhabitants and they hauled them about town, &c.

Jan. 20 This day delivered all the schooner *Manchester*'s blocks and ties, viz. two ties, 1 mainstay, twelve blocks, 1 boom pendent. This day the inhabitants tarred and feathered the four men that went to Cat Island and carried them to Salem and back again.

* * * * *

Jan. 23 This day so cold no sermon this forenoon. We are advised this afternoon to not fall out by the way side [?] and will mob the mob[?].

Jan. 24 This day a full Town Meeting about the hospital at Cat Island. A committee chosen. Smart cold. Do nothing at loft.

Jan. 25. This day smart cold. A child of Thompson moved to Ferry [with] smallpox. Deliver some of the *Hawk*'s rigging to the mate.

Jan. 26 This day somewhat cold. This night the hospital took fire and was consumed with barn, little [?] house and all. Died a child, Thompson, at Ferry.

* * * * *

Feb. 25 This day fine and moderate. Delivered a tie to schooner *Hannah*, Phollet. Delivered two tackle blocks to schooner *Eagle*, Brus. Delivered a jibsheet straps to schooner *Betsey*, Gatchell. This day the Proprietors of Essex Hospital took two men up on suspicion of their being concerned in burning the hospital at Cat Island and carried them to Salem and put them in prison, but our fishermen all rose in a body and went to Salem and brought them home again. One of them is John Watts; other J[ohn] Guillard. [Another account by Bowen reads:] This day at noon the leather-breeches soul-catcher came to town and catched two of Simon Peter's children out of their ships and carried them to the City. As soon as Andrew and their brethren knew of it, they all forsook their ships and followed them in a great multitude and went to the City and relieved their two brethren and conducted them safe to their habitations again. There was a watch set. All is well. Died a child [of] S. Baker's [at] Ferry.

Feb. 26 This day fine and pleasant. Puddened an anchor for Mr. John Griste. Delivered two blocks to schooner *Eagle*, Brus, and a jibstay to Captain White. Arrived A[lexander] Ross from Cadiz [in the schooner *Tabby*]. The Proprietors of Essex Hospital buried the hatchet forever.

Feb. 27 This day moderate. Some snow fell the last night. Attend to Church all day. Sailed [Michael] Merrick [in the schooner *Betsey* for Lisbon, William] Sinclair [in the schooner *Betsey* for Barbados], and [John] Hooper [in the schooner *Lynn* for Bilbao]. Arrived Ben Boden in schooner *Nancy* from the Mediterranean [Lematt]. Sailed [Michael] Dupee in [the schooner] *Absalom* [for the West Indies].

Monday, Feb. 28 This day do nothing at loft. Delivered two blocks to schooner *Eagle*, Brus. Sailed some of our fishermen. This day a noise [with] the High Sheriff at Salem about something. All is well. Finis for the Isle Cat.

3. Excerpts from the *Essex Gazette* Relating to the Smallpox Epidemic and Inoculation Controversy (1773–74)

[The *Essex Gazette*, founded in 1768 and published in Salem, was the only newspaper in Essex County at the time of the smallpox episode. As one can quickly tell, the editors were sympathetic to the inoculation cause and hostile to those residents of Marblehead, such as Bowen, who were opposed to the hospital. The phrase "this town" in its pages refers to Salem, not Marblehead.]

July 20–27 We hear from Marblehead, that two Persons lately had the Small-Pox in that Town, and recovered, before it was suspected that they had the Disease, attributing their Eruptions and Sickness to some Kind of Poison which they had inadvertently taken. Those persons were occasionally visited, during the Course of their Disorder, by a Number of Persons who were liable to catch the Small-Pox. Several of these Persons breaking out with it, the latter End of last Week, was the first Discovery the Inhabitants made of the Danger they were exposed to, which occasioned great Consternation in the Town, as, at a moderate Computation, it contains not less than five or six Thousand Persons subject to receive that disease. We have the Pleasure, however, to hear, that, by the careful and vigilant Conduct of the Selectmen, under God, there is at present no great Danger of it spreading.

MARBLEHEAD, July 26, 1773

July 27–Aug. 3 THE SELECTMEN of MARBLEHEAD hereby notify the Publick That the Small-Pox is but in one House in the Town, which is a Quarter of a Mile below the Market-House, and close to the Water-Side—And in two Houses at the Ferry, one Mile from the Market-House.—No other Place in Town being infected with that Distemper, (a Committee of Inspection daily examining every House in Town) Travellers and Market-Men may come as usual, and be in no Danger of any Infection at Present.

Aug. 3–10 The Selectmen of Marblehead hereby assure the Publick [as of 2 August] That the Small-Pox is in but one House in Town, which is the House where it first broke out: That all the Persons who have broke out with that Distemper, for a Fortnight past, are all removed to the back Side of the Town, one Mile from the Market. The House, which is infected in the Town, is fenced up ... and there is a great Probability that no more Persons will be taken down with the Distemper.

Aug. 10–17 The Town of Marblehead having made Application for Liberty to erect an inoculating Hospital on Cat-Island, within the Jurisdiction of this Town [Salem], a Meeting of the Inhabitants was held Yesterday for considering the same. It appeared by the Debates that they were generally sensible of the Utility of such a Hospital's being established; but a Doubt arose respecting the Propriety, Safety or Legality of adopting or prosecuting a Measure of that Kind by any less Authority than an Act of the Legislature. A Vote was accordingly passed to this Effect: That the Inhabitants of this Town are content that the Town of Marblehead, or any Inhabitants thereof, should erect an Hospital on Cat-Island, for Inoculating for the Small-Pox, provided they first obtain Leave of the General Court.

Aug. 17–24 The Select-Men of Marblehead hereby assure the Publick That there is no Person now sick with the Small-Pox in the Town; that the House where the Infection first broke out, is now cleansing: That all Persons who are taken down with the Distemper are immediately removed to some Houses which are situate on the Back of the Town, a Mile from the Market-House ... That daily Search and Inspection is made among the Inhabitants, so that every Person who is taken with the Distemper is removed before he becomes infectious ... N.B. Only five Persons have broke out the Week past.

We hear that a fishing Vessel arrived at Marblehead last Friday, and brought in about 270 Quintals of Fish; the People of whom, or some of them, before they sailed from that Place, had been in the House where the Small-Pox first broke out, before it was known 'twas that Distemper, and on the Voyage they all had that Disease without suspecting what it was, & one of them (a Boy) died of it; they afterwards found themselves so weak and poorly that they were obliged to get a Cape-Ann Vessel[1] to spare them two Hands to bring them in.

Sept. 14–21 The Select-Men of Marblehead hereby notify the Publick [as of 20 September] That the House where the Small-Pox first broke out is now cleansed; the Fences which fenced it in, are taken down, and People pass and repass as usual. There has but one Person been taken down with the Distemper this Fortnight, and there are only three but what are recovered.

Sept. 21–28 The Select-Men of Marblehead hereby notify the Publick [as of 27 September] That the Town is entirely clear of the Small-Pox, and that only one Person has it at the Ferry, above a Mile from the Town.

Oct. 19–26 On Tuesday last the first Class of Patients went down to the Essex Hospital. As a Number of respectable Persons of both Sexes were in it, and the Hospital was clear of Infection, many Gentlemen of the Town accompanied it to the Island, and the Hospital was thronged in every Quarter. In the Afternoon, the House was cleared, and Doctor Jackson proceeded to inoculate the Patients, being One Hundred and Three in Number. Doctor [Ananais] Randall was unexpectedly detained 'till towards the Evening.—The Patents are daily displaying their Signal of Health from the Middle of the Island, and all are in high Spirits.

Nov. 2–9 On Friday Evening last the Patients of Essex Hospital commemorated the happy Deliverance of the English Nation from the GUN-POWDER PLOT. Tar Barrels on the Occasion were ordered from the Town, and a large Fire displayed from the Middle of the Island; the Hospital was likewise illuminated, and made a most beautiful Appearance here. Rockets were ordered from Boston, but happening rather the latest for the Hospital, a Number of Gentlemen, who spent the Evening at the Assembly Room, had them played off from their

---

1 Cape-Ann vessel meant a fishing vessel from Gloucester—Marblehead's main competition in the fishery.

Quarters, and spent the Evening after very jovially, as did their Friends and Acquaintances under Inoculation.

Nov. 9–16 On Thursday Evening died at the Essex Hospital, of a nervous Fever, *Sarah Roads*, aged 15 years. The circumstances of her Death were as follows: Avery Clark, a young Woman who heretofore had had the Small Pox, was employed by the Proprietors as a Waiter to the Hospital; she was soon after her coming to the Hospital seized with a nervous Fever; which she had to a very great Degree. This Deceased came to the Hospital to be inoculated, and afterwards to serve as Nurse; for Want of Room and other Convenience, she was obliged to lodge with the above young Woman, during part of her Sickness. She went through the Small-Pox, which she had equally favourable with any in the Hospital, not having more than twenty Pustules, and those of the mildest Kind, in her Face, and a less Proportion in her Body. During the whole Time she did the business of a Nurse in the Hospital, until about six Days before her Death she was seized with a Pain in her Head, Back and Limbs; a violent Fever and Delirium came on; and notwithstanding she had the united Consultation and Advice of six Physicians, was obliged to submit to the Stroke of Death. The above Avery Clark is on the Recovery.

Jan. 11–18 We learn from Marblehead that considerable Disturbance arose in that Town last Week with Respect to the landing a Number of Patients from the Essex Hospital. It seems, as we hear, that they were coming ashore at a different Place from that lately voted by the Town for their Landing; whereupon a considerable Number of the Inhabitants mustered, and beat or pushed them off two or three Times; and the Patients were at Length obliged to look for another Landing-Place.

Jan. 18–25 Last Week four Men belonging to Marblehead were suspected, by some Circumstances in the Behaviour, of having a Design of attempting to steal a Quantity of Cloathing from the Essex Hospital; they were accordingly watched; and on Wednesday Night last, on their Return from the Island, were pursued and taken. It appeared that they had picked up a Quantity of Cloathing, near the Hospital, that was put out for airing: But, on their Return to the Town, finding themselves pursued by several Boats, threw a considerable Part of it overboard. Their Persons being secured until the next Day, Thursday, a large Body of Mobility assembled; when it was determined, by a great Majority, that the Mode of Punishment should be *Tarring* and *Feathering*—In Consequence of this Determination, the most extraordinary Exhibition of the Kind, ever seen in North-America, was drawn forth to public View. The Procession formed, on Thursday Morning, at the Town-House in

Marblehead. The four Objects of Resentment were placed in a Cart, facing each other, having been previously tarred and feathered in the modern Way. A Fifer and one Drummer were placed in the Front of the Carriage, which according to the Computation of some Persons, was preceded by one thousand People, chiefly dressed in Uniform, among whom were four Drummers. In this manner they marched from Marblehead to Salem, 4½ miles, and entered the Town about 12 o'Clock. Here, forming a Junction with a numerous Body of the Inhabitants, they paraded through the principal Streets, with Drums beating, a Fife playing, and a large white Flag flying from the Cart, which, with the exquisitely droll and grotesque Appearance of the four tarred and feathered Objects of Derision, exhibited a very laughable and truly comic Scene. They went out of the Town before one o'Clock, and returned to Marblehead, where they dispersed.

Jan. 25–Feb. 1 On Monday, last Week, a Meeting was called at Marblehead, to put a Stop to the Disorders which for several Days before had happened in the Place. As the Dispute respected the Essex Hospital, it was agreed by the Proprietors to shut it up; and at their Desire a Committee of the Town was chosen to inspect the cleaning of Furniture, Apparel, &c. On Tuesday the Committee went to the Hospital, and attended their Business until Wednesday Night, when they awaked with the Rest of the Family, being eleven in Number, surrounded with Flames. The Ruffians who perpetrated this Act, went from the Town prepared with Tar Tubs, &c. and proceeded setting Fire to all Parts of the House without any Attempt to awake the People. So infernal were the Villains that they struck down one Man who in Amazement had jumped from his Bed, and was running from the Flames. The Steward had a Blow from another of them with an Andiron; it was aimed at his Head, but happily missing it, took his Shoulder, and brought him to the Floor. One of the Patients, with a Child at her Breast, was driven to the Smoke-House, fainting several Times as she went. And others were turned out, cold as it was, with scarcely any Thing to cover them.—The Perpetrators are not yet apprehended.—The Town is in such Confusion that a military Watch is nightly kept, as it's thought Lives and Properties are not safe without it. The above Account we received from a Correspondent; in Addition to which, we hear, that the Number of People who went over to Cat-Island, to burn the Hospital, was about 20; Part of them, in Disguise, went up from where they landed, and set Fire to the Building, which contained 70 Beds, with Bedding, and all the other Furniture belonging to the Hospital, the whole of which was consumed, together with a Barn.—

The loss to the Proprietors (four in Number) is estimated at Two Thousand Pounds L[awful] M[oney].[1]

Feb. 8–15 We hear that a Petition was preferred to the General Court, a few days since, by a Number of the principal Inhabitants of Marblehead, setting forth the Great Confusion that Town is in, occasioned by the lawless Proceedings of a Number of Persons in burning the Hospital there, committing other Acts of Violence, and by their Threats of doing further Mischief: And praying such speedy Relief as the Court may in their Wisdom, should see meet. Upon which a Committee of the two Houses was appointed to repair to Marblehead to enquire into the Grounds of the Uneasiness subsisting there.

Feb. 22–Mar. 1 Last Friday, in the Forenoon, Mr. [Nathan] Brown of this Place [Salem], Deputy-Sheriff, went on board a fishing Vessel, at Marblehead, and arrested John Watts and John Guillard, in an Action of Damages for £3000, commenced by the Gentlemen who were Proprietors of the late Essex Hospital, on Suspicion that the said two Persons were concerned in Burning that Building on the 26th of January last.—The Prisoners were commited to his Majesty's Goal [*sic*] in this Town about 2 o'Clock, P.M. Almost as soon as the Keys were turned upon them, the People began, in small Companies, to enter the Town from Marblehead, and continued coming over in this Manner till near Night, rendezvouzing near the Goal. The Magistrates were busy consulting upon Measures for preserving the Peace, and for dispersing the People who were assembled from Marblehead; from whence a still greater Number was expected after Dark. About Sunset, on Application to the Colonel of the Militia, the Drums were ordered out, and beat *To Arms*.—Immediately upon hearing this, the Mob, to the Number of 4 or 500, arming themselves with Clubs, Sticks of Wood, &c. and while it was yet Day-Light, made a most furious Attack on the Goal.—They first burst open the Doors, and broke most of the lower Windows in that Part of the Building which is the Prison-Keeper's Dwelling; and then, with Iron Crows, Axes, &c. they soon beat their Way through four of the Prison-Doors, each of which was very strong, and well secured with many large Locks. Thus, having got into two Apartments of the Prison, in less than 10 minutes, from the first Onset, carried off the abovementioned two Prisoners in Triumph, and went immediately to Marblehead, where they soon dispersed. They assembled again the next Day, and

---

1 Lawful Money refers to the Massachusetts currency that had been issued since 1751, as opposed to earlier issues (termed "Old Tenor") or British sterling currency.

obliged the Gentlemen abovementioned to declare that no Prosecutions should ever be commenced on Account of burning the Hospital.

Mar. 1–8 In Consequence of the Rescue of the two Prisoners ... the High Sheriff of the County, on Monday Afternoon, last Week, gave orders to his Deputy in this Town [Salem] to command the Inhabitants to meet in School Street at 9 o'Clock the next Morning, with Arms and Ammunition according to Law, to assist the High Sheriff in the Execution of his Office; in Pursuance of which Orders, several Hundred were commanded to appear.—This body, when assembled, was to march to Marblehead, and assist the Sheriff in retaking the said Prisoners, as well as to apprehend the Principals concerned in breaking into the Goal. On the other Hand, it was given out, that the Marblehead People, to the Number of 6 or 800, were arming and were determined to repel, to the last Extremity, any Force that should be brought against them. In this critical Situation of Things, a Number of the principal Gentlemen of Marblehead were happily instrumental in effecting a Compromise; the Proprietors of the late Essex Hospital being influenced to relinquish all Demands that they might have either on the County or Sheriff, in Consequence of the Rescue and Escape of the abovementioned Prisoners, and to discontinue all Proceedings respecting the burning of the Hospital. This measure, which restored Peace, was reported abroad just before the Time at which the People were ordered to assemble and was the Cause of much Joy and Satisfaction to the Town in general.

Mar. 29–Apr. 5 We hear from Marblehead, that a Person named Clark, went to Cat-Island last Wednesday and took away some Cloaths, (said to be his own) which he brought up to the Town. As they had been infected with the Small-Pox, and it was uncertain whether they were cleansed or not, he was immediately ordered, by the Selectmen, round to the Ferry, back of the Town, where the Cloaths were to be examined. he accordingly obeyed: But returning to Town again, he was surrounded by a considerable Number of People; and lest they should proceed to any Violence with him, the Selectmen appeared, and promised that he should be properly and legally punished, if deserving of it, the next Day. This seemed to satisfy the People: But about 10 or 11 o'Clock at Night, 20 or 30 of them went and pulled him out of his House, carried him to the public Whipping-Post, and whipped him most cruelly. The next day he went to Ipswich, made his Complaint to the Justices of the Inferior Court, then sitting, and told who the Persons were that abused him. A Warrant was issued, one of the Criminals were taken up and committed to Goal, and a good Look-Out is kept for apprehending the others; one of whom, as he was returning from Meeting on the last Sabbath, an Officer gave Chace to, but could not catch him.—The abovementioned Clark is one of the Persons who were tarred and feathered some Time since.

4. Ashley Bowen, Journal Entries Relating to the Smallpox Epidemic (1777)

[This material comes from Bowen's "Day Book and Journal (1775–1777)," owned by the American Antiquarian Society in Worcester, Massachusetts, and is excerpted from Smith, ed., *Journals of Ashley Bowen*, 45: 516–21.]

Apr. 13 This day close weather. Wind southerly. Many of our town's folk are moved with smallpox. Old Mrs. Clune died at pox house. Most of the disorder layeth at the lower end of the town, and they are moved to Pitman's house &c.

Apr. 14 This day much wind at NW. A Town Meeting about smallpox. Chose a Committee of Safety.

Apr. 15 This morning cold. Much wind at WNW. Sundry persons broke out with smallpox. Came to town 50 bus[hels] of Indian meal as a donation for poor poor. Sailed Grush for West Indies

Apr. 16 This day fair weather. I dined at Captain Prince farm. Tis said more troops are coming from England [and] West Indies. Sall Johnson.

Apr. 17 This day close weather. Wind easterly. The smallpox seems to be abated. Many of our town folk are gone to Sewell's Point to be pockalated. Sall Johnson went yesterday. Elizabeth Hudson died of smallpox.

Apr. 18 This day close weather. Arrived William Boyles from West Indies. Our smallpox seems to abate.

Apr. 19 This day [...].

Apr. 20 This day wind easterly. Passed a ship and sloop for Boston from sea and a brig from Salem for Boston. Much rain.

Apr. 21 This day foggy. Moderate. A Town Meeting and are to inoculate. A committee chose for to get doctors.

Apr. 22 This day fine and pleasant. We hear Captain Nicholas Gordon is arrive at Portsmouth. I dined at the farm. Three people are dead at Major Pedrick house. Came to town ‹Doctor Hall Jackson›.

Apr. 23 This day some fog. Tis said that two of King George's ships are a-cruising off Cape Ann and St. George's Bay. Employed at the farm. Tabitha Bartol, widow, removed from Mr. H[enry] Sanders. They dies fast with smallpox at the Pesthouse.

* * * * *

Apr. 28 This day anchored here John Hodges from Bilbao in schooner [...]. This morning the bell man went about town to inform inhabitants that inoculation will take place on Wednesday next through the town.

Apr. 29 This day moderate. Cold. This afternoon the lower part of this town began to inoculate.

Apr. 30 This day our inoculation gentry have inoc[ulat]ed as far up as Captain Gerry's. Died Isaac Martin at Sewell's Point with smallpox and John Lyon's wife in town. Pox hath entered the town. Tis said the British troops have landed.

May 1 This day much rain. A mock Fast Day with the Yankees. No preaching nor prayer. This evening Captain James Mugford was inoculated. Our sister Stiles was inoculated with Captain Mugford family.

May 2 This day fair and pleasant. At ten o'clock my four children were inoculated, viz. son Ashley, daughters Hannah, Molly, and Sarah Ashley. At eleven o'clock Captain Edward Bowen's family were inoculated. Phil [Le]Craw wife died. Sailed Bartholomew Jackson

May 3 Moderate. Nothing a-doing but smallpox work.

May 4 This morning I went to attend the lines at Elish[a] Gathell's. Passed into town William Lee, Esq. At noon this afternoon passed into town Major Sprague's wife and two children to be inoculated. Sailed for Bilbao John Harris in schooner.

May 5 This day much rain. I attended the smokehouse till night. Much rain. Came in Richard Dixey from Baltimore with flour. Captain Prince's three children were inoculated at town, viz. Nancy, Joseph, and Hannah. Came to town Captain Foster [who] brought his nigger and child to be inoculated.

May 6 This day moderate. Sally Johnson and Nathan Martin came from Sewell's Point. A Town Meeting &c. At noon died Mrs. Orne, the wife of Joshua Orne, merchant, and this night died Mrs. Homan, wife of Mr. Edward Homan, cooper. Pox.

May 7 This night wind SE. Some rain. Mrs. Orne and Homan was buried. No bells tolled for either death. The bells are not to toll during inoculation.

May 8 This day close weather. Some rain. The *True Blue* and *Bellona* bent their sails this afternoon. The remains of Mr. Nathaniel Homan was buried.

May 9 This morning wind easterly. We find a brig ashore on Tinker's Island and a ship at anchor without the Pig Rocks.[1] Much rain.

May 10 This day close weather. Passed two sloops from sea for Salem and passed three brigs from Salem for Boston. Mr. Benjamin Boden, Town Clerk, was brought into town with smallpox. Our inoculated folk are all in good spirits. Great talk of a fleet of ships coming from England.

May 11 This day wind easterly. Mr. Samuel Chapman came in with smallpox. Our children in a good way.

May 12 This day moderate. Wind SE. John Martin went to Tinker's Island and brought the Frenchman's goods that was saved from the wreck &c. Came to town upward of 100 people from all quarter to be inoculated. Heavenly Times Brother Dick!

May 13 This day cold for the times. Many coasting vessels off and about Cape Ann. Died Mrs. Charity Phillips, widow, &c. Our streets are as full of strange faces as when the port of honest Boston was first shut up in the first of June, 1774. TEA and toast. Note: we have some of the noble clergy of many towns round and about and in town.

May 14 This day moderate The last night I watched with Mr. B[enjamin] Boden. Many guns fired at Boston. We hear the *Tyrannicide* hath a prize into Portsmouth. Sailed a small schooner for a spy, John Hines, master.

May 15 This day pleasant for the times. A pock-a-times of it &c.

May 16 This day some rain.

May 17 This day fine and moderate wind at NW. At noon died Mrs. Ashton and Samuel Ashton, the schoolmaster's wife. Passed a topsail schooner for Boston. Came to town the Honorable Robert Hooper and is inoculated. All well.

May 18 This day moderate wind s-easterly. Anchored here the ship *American Tartar*, Captain J[oh]n Grimes, from Boston.

May 19 Close weather. Some rain. Passed a brig and topsail sloop from Boston. Died Mrs. Bond, smallpox. Town Meeting for Representative &c. Died Charles Dunn's wife. Died 2 white, 1 black children.

May 20 This day moderate. Died Mrs. Nicholas Bartlett and Mrs. Ashton, widow. Died Molly Stone.

---

1 Tinker's Island and Pig Rocks are both off the south end of Marblehead Neck and are still considered a danger to shipping.

May 21 This day pleasant. At 2 o'clock sailed John Manley Esq. and two ships and 9 other vessels more from Nantasket for sea. Wind SSW; hauled off EbS. And at 4 o'clock sailed from here the ships [*American*] *Tartar* for Cape Ann. We hear two frigates are off belonging to King George &c.

May 22 This morning at eight o'clock passed a fleet of shipping, viz. three ships and eight brigs and schooner. Note: Admiral Mathews led the van and Admiral Lestock kept the rear and they lay off and on all day. At noon the [*American*] *Tartar* joined the fleet. The last night died Captain John Reed, an old sea commander, and Joseph Mecoloathey [*sic*]. Died the wife of William Nick Junior.

May 23 This day moderate and warm. No ships off. The last night I watched with Mr. [Benjamin] Boden. Four grown people buried, viz. Captain Reed, Mrs. Ashton, Mrs. Nick, a woman belonging to Salem. Our fishermen heard many cannon off in the Bay. Died a lad, Collins.

May 24 This day fine and warm. Employed on Colonel Jonathan Glover's shrouds. This night died Mr. Nath[anie]l Holder, the wife of Mr. Benjamin Homan, cooper, P[eter] Bonner Jayne, and died Mrs. Jane Bridges. Altered a pendent for Captain John Selman.

May 25 This day fine and warm but rather hot for the pox. Mame Bowen not so well as was expected. Both our spies are out &c. This afternoon three funerals. Tis said John Hooper is dead—Johnny Hooper.

May 26 This day wind east. Anchored here Captain John Dev[ereux?] Dennis[?] This night many of the inhabitants broke out afresh with smallpox. Died Simpson Boden and old Mrs. Lewis. Died John Bubier of consumption and Mr. Samuel Brimblecome by inoculation.

May 27 This day much wind easterly. Some rain. Parson Weeks's house took fire but timely discovered and put out.[1] John Bubier and Glover's Jack buried. Many persons are taking the smallpox the natural way, some after they have been twice inoculated. Fine times &c.!

5. Ashley Bowen, Journal Entries on Minding the Smokehouse During the Smallpox Epidemic (1792)

[Immersion in dense sulfur smoke inside a smokehouse was thought by some to prevent the spread of smallpox. Bowen had minded the watchhouse, where travelers were probably smoked, on the Boston

---

1 Joshua Weeks was the Anglican minister of St. Michael's Anglican Church in Marblehead and a strong Loyalist.

Road during the smallpox epidemic in 1764. In 1792, in his retirement from active labor, he was asked to perform the duty once again. This material comes from Smith, ed., *Journals of Ashley Bowen*, 45: 582, 583–84.]

Sept. 10 This day I agreed with the Selectmen to take charge of the smokehouse near the Widow Gatchell's with Aaron Tucker Huy as an assistant and smoked it on the first evening and a stranger.

★ ★ ★ ★ ★

Sept. 29 This evening came John Skinner from Boston and smoked and Captains Trevett and Cowell, both smoked. At midnight came from Boston a coach-full of men. Some were smoked and some not. A hubbub, and they broke the lock of the gate and went through to town. Sunday morning at 6 o'clock I went to town and complained of the coachman and passengers and found the coach in a barn that Mrs. Warner puts carriages in, and then I called up Mr. Knott Pedrick and next Captain Sam Hooper, then Squire Sewall and then Colonel W[illiam] R[aymond] Lee. Captain Foster unwell. I called Mr. Robert Hooper up, and then I went towards Mr. Sewall's and Captain Sam Hooper sent me to call Mr. [Marston] Watson, and then I went to Mrs. Warner's and found the Selectmen all there. I went back and forward the entry, but our Selectmen said nothing to me but heard a man story. What he said I am not able to say, and when the Selectmen came out of Mrs. Warner's I asked Captain Hooper if I might get my breakfast, and after breakfast I came to the gate again.

[Another account of the episode follows:] Memorandum of Saturday night September the 29 P.M. and 30 A.M., 1792. Late in the evening came from Boston Captain Sam Trevett and R. Cowell and were smoked. Afterwards came a coach. Note: after Trevett and Cowell went in I turned out and let one cob and another cart out and then I turned in again and soon after I heard a carriage on Boston Road. I said to Tucker, "Turn out and see who was coming." And he said, "A coach and they said from Boston." And I turned out and said, "Where from?" And they said, "From Boston." I said, "You must be smoke[d]," and I ordered Tucker to prepare a smoke. And two of the passenger and the coachman came and entered the smoke apartment but would not let me shut the door, and they came out, and I desired them to smoke their hats, which they did, and the coachman smoke his cushions. And then

I went to inquire the state of the coach and found two men that had not been set off the coach, and the first man that was smoked I find was named Prince and stood spokesman and said he would go in. I said if I was satisfied they should, but I must have all smoked, and the second two men went into the outer room and came out again and said, "The old fellow hath an Hell! Let us see how he likes it!" And one of them came and took me by the arm and said, "Come and smoke us!" I dreaded the consequence and said if the two men would come out I would smoke them. Tucker was at the gate, but I said, "Keep fast the gate!" and he gave me the key, and one of them said there was no business for a fence [there] and "Break the gate open!" And as Tucker stood by the gate one of them went to him and took him by the arm and hauled him from the gate and forced the lock open and opened the gate. And then I took my hat and sat off for Town and run off around Bubier Plains and the coach overtook me and I turned back and tarried till dawning and then I went to Town and called up all the Selectmen but Captain Foster, and they met at Warner's.

Appendix D: Ashley Bowen, Journal Entries During the American Revolution

[These entries were selected from a number of day books and interleaved almanacs, which Bowen kept during the Revolutionary War. The entire text of his original accounts covering the period can be found in Smith, ed., *Journals of Ashley Bowen*, 45: 394–550.]

1. The Coercive Acts Take Effect (1774)

[Source: Smith, ed., *Journals of Ashley Bowen*, 45: 394, 396–97, 398–99, 400, 404.]

May, 1774. Arrived His Britannic Majesty Ship *Lively*, Captain [Thomas] Bishop, with Thomas Gage Esq. appointed Governor of Massachusetts-Bay, New England. Admiral Montague in His Majesty Ship *Captain* laying at Boston and a number of frigates.

★ ★ ★ ★ ★

May 13 This day do little at loft. We hear great guns fire at Boston; suppose the new Governor is come. Arrived General Thomas Gage for to be Governor of Boston. A woman, [the wife of B. Thompson,] moved with smallpox. Arrived [William] Sinclair [in the schooner *Betsey*] from Barbados.

★ ★ ★ ★ ★

May 25 This morning I heard a number of cannon fired, I suppose at Boston, and at 1 o'clock P.M. I heard firing at Boston. Tis supposed that there is not one black negro slave in this town, but many white are in town this day. This day is High Election. This evening some rain.

The firing of cannon was due to the election of H.M. Councillors for the Province.

★ ★ ★ ★ ★

May 31 This day great To-Do at Boston. Great doings at Boston by their firing so many guns. The two and thirty day of May. Terrible times in Tarsa[?].

June 1 The Port of Boston blocked up by the British and 14 days allowed the merchants to sail for the port of Marblehead as a free port, and all the wood coasters were ordered here to Marblehead and examined before they could go to Boston.[1] There was soldiers planted here and guard boats. The Custom House was here and goods were sent to Boston by land and our streets filled with strange faces and Boston full of British troops. Sad Times! J.C.A. [Jesus Christ Almighty?] Note: Admiral Montague sailed July the 8. Admiral Graves arrived July the 1.

This day we saw 3 ships of war go to Boston. At noon anchored here a ship from Bristol, Captain Williamson. Sailed N[icholas] B[artlett Jr.] and D[avid] Ross [in the brig *Union*]. Note: Major Duncan and Captain Ferguson come passengers. Our street full of tide waiters and other officers as Boston is blocked up.

* * * * *

June 14 This day is the last day of letting out of any merchantmen from the port of Boston. This morning anchored here a large new double-deck schooner from Boston for Quebec, McNeill, master. Sailed brig [*Rambler*, Cabot,] for Quebec. We hear four thousand troops were land yesterday on Long Wharf, Boston. Arrived Richard James [in the schooner *Hannah*] from West Indies [Barbados]. Returned Jeremiah Lee from Baltimore. Many woodmen in our harbour.

* * * * *

June 24 This day arrived a brig and two double-decked schooners and a double-deck sloop. Some rain. Sailed John Gale [in the schooner *Hannah* for the West Indies]. The body of a man drove up on Bartlett Beach. A Jury of Inquest sat on him and [he] was buried. This evening the remains of Mr. Joseph Carder was buried. Sailed many woodmen for Boston. Note: the woodmen are obliged to have on board two

---

1 The Boston Port Act, one of the four Coercive Acts passed by the British Parliament in 1774, closed the port of Boston to all imports save food until the tea that had been destroyed in the Tea Party of the previous fall was paid for.

soldiers and a tidewaiter[1] when they go to Boston. The soldiers are landed at the Castle and the tidewaiter discharged at their arrival at the town of Boston and walk home.

* * * * *

Aug. 1 This day the most friendly people to the town of Boston sent 11 wagons' load of the riches of the Banks [226 quintals Jamaica fish], one cask of the fatness of Spain [oil], some cash &c., to the relief of the Poor Poor of the town of Boston. D[eacon Samuel] G[atchell] the commander-in-chief of the wagons. Note: our wagons are our own common carts, ten of them, and one belonging to Lynn. Our carters give half their fees. Sailed a brig for Plymouth. Arrived Philip Thrash [from] Lisbon. Delivered 4 pair of topmast shrouds and a pair of backstays to brig *St. Paul.* Sailed Sam Green [in the schooner *Hitty*] for West Indies. Captain Mathews, his mark ↑ ·

2. Lexington and Concord (1775)

[Source: Smith, ed., *Journals of Ashley Bowen*, 45: 435–36.]

Apr. 19, 1775 A hubbub as no truth goes. A hubbub about soldiers.[2] News from afar talks of war. Employed on schooner *Patty*'s blocks. Sailed schooner *Patty*, Will Clark, [whaleman]. Employed Dennin 6 hours. Sailed William Sinclair for Europe.

Apr. 20 Do nothing at loft, but delivered a suit of rigging to Captain Is[rael] Foster for a brig. Passed a ship for Salem from London, Callahan, master. Arrived ship here.

Apr. 21 This day moderate. Arrived brig *Woodbridge.* I was taken on board the *Lively* but acquitted.[3] His Majesty Ship *Lively* bent sails. Arrived Pote from Guadaloupe.

Apr. 22 His Majesty ship *Lively* block our harbor up and sent a message on shore. A meeting at the Town House. Father Bowen took his flight to farm. Arrived R. Hinkley.

---

1 A tidewaiter was a customs officer who awaited the arrival of ships (formerly coming in with the tide), and boarded them to prevent evasion of the customs-house regulations.

2 This was Bowen's only reference to the battles of Lexington and Concord.

3 Why Bowen was taken on board this British naval vessel and why he was released remain a mystery, but he may well have been impressed and then released possibly on account of his age (47 years).

Apr. 23 Much firing at Boston. Fog. Self at Church all day. War's no dependence on anything; between two stools the ass comes to the ground.

Apr. 24 This day moderate. Dull, dull, dull times. Sister Stiles gone in the country. No business in hand. Between King and Country.

3. Bunker Hill (1775)

[From Bowen's report, one would think this was an American defeat. Source: Smith, ed., *Journals of Ashley Bowen*, 45: 444, 445].

June 13 This day passed sixteen ships and two brigs for Boston, all transports from England, some with horse and some with troops on board. The small tender sailed for Boston. Anchored a small brig from Lisbon. Came from Boston John Brock in Jacob Fowle schooner.

★ ★ ★ ★ ★

June 16 Sailed four ships from Boston for sea. Sailed [schooner] Captain Leaton for Salem. General Putnam is a-trenching on Bunker's Hill at Charlestown.

June 17 This day the *Merlin* firing at a target. This morning the King's troops set fire to Charlestown and came under cover of the smoke and attacked the intrenchments on Bunker Hill and caused them to retreat. Sail small brig for Boston.

June 18 Some likely hoods for rueing all sins fail in a daytime [?] This day much firing at Boston &c. Tis said a great number of men are killed on both sides.

★ ★ ★ ★ ★

Aug. 19 This day fair weather. [Nothing new.] I sold Mr. Henry Sanders 1 [hundred weight] 3 [quarters] 14 of hay. This afternoon passed by a ship and sloop from Boston towards Cape Ann. Poor Marblehead is threatened by the Headquarters of a visit from that quarter if we let any of the King's men land or supply them with even water. Only between two stools our ass comes to the grounds. Poor, poor, oh poor Marblehead!

4. Benedict Arnold's Attack on Quebec (1775–76)

[Arnold's expedition against Quebec was an American disaster. Source: Smith, ed., *Journals of Ashley Bowen*, 45: 456, 474.]

Sept. 19, 1775 Foggy morning. Sailed two ships from Boston. Latter part, cloudy. Sailed the Canadian [?] fleet

★ ★ ★ ★ ★

Jan. 20, 1776 This day smart cold. News from Quebec as cold. The news from Quebec is not for the good of the Colonies. Tis said 7 seamen are killed by the landsmen at Manchester. I hope not so.

5. Two Weeks in the War (1776)

[In Bowen's view, and probably that of many other coastal inhabitants, it was the movements of ships and the threat from the British Navy rather than the reports of military maneuvers on land that mattered most. Source: Smith, ed., *Journals of Ashley Bowen*, 45: 488–90.]

June 3 This day close weather. Sailed sundry vessels for Boston. A man broke out with smallpox on board the sloop *Yankee*. Anchored here the schooner *Lee*, Waters [captain?], and this evening anchored Tucker. I bought a ¼ of a barrel of fresh beef.

June 4 This day fair weather. Lay here the Continental cruisers.[1] My son Ashley came to town yesterday and sat off again today a-roving.[2]

June 5 This day sailed Waters in schooner *Lee* and Johnson in sloop *Yankee* and Tucker in schooner *Hancock*. Sailed from below Boston a large ship. Anchored here schooner *Warren*, O'Burke. The schooner *Franklin* at Boston. Came from Ipswich Major Pedrick schooner, [...] fisherman to land her fish.

June 6 This day fair, warm. This forenoon I went to Salem. This afternoon I saw three cruiser off Cape Ann. Tis said a ship is gone in to Cape Ann Harbor.

---

1 These cruisers, including the *Warren*, *Hancock*, *Lee*, *Franklin*, and *Lynch*, were armed schooners commissioned by George Washington to prey on British shipping.

2 A-roving meant privateering—that is, preying with a license from one's own government on enemy shipping.

June 7 This day fair weather. Tis said the ship is from Jamaica for London. Tis said the *Yankee Hero* of Newbury hath taken a Scotch prize off Cape Ann. All our cruisers are out in pursuit of a ship from Glasgow with troops on board.

June 8 This morning the schooners *Warren* and *Lee* came in to this harbor of Marblehead with their true prize from Glasgow in Scotland and with 95 Highland troops. The ship is the *Ann*, Captain [John] Denniston, five weeks and 6 days out. Passed the *Milford* and *Yankee Hero* her prize for the lighthouse.

June 9 The last evening I came on board the ship *Ann* in order to cleanse her from the smallpox with Captain Roads, Eli[as] Vickery, Thomas Antiton and Jam[es] Quilty, and this day unbent ship's sails and carried the sick to Cat Island and landed the sails at Nick's Cove. Burke engaged a ship and bark. Waters lay in our harbor all day. Came a brig from below Boston and carried a schooner in and the ship and bark. Note: Captain Samuel Green hath the charge of the ship *Ann*.

June 10 This day on board ship *Ann*. Carried all the bedding and other clothing to Cat Island that was between decks and washed all clean between decks.

June 11 This day we carried all the boards on shore to the Neck and burnt them, and then we smoked the ship and washed her with vinegar from stem to stern. The men are erecting a fort on Hewett's Head.

June 12 This day on board ship *Ann*. Employed in attend in clearing the cabin and steerage, and this forenoon a King's brig chased three sloop that came from Boston. This afternoon four of our cruiser chased the brig into the lighthouse, and then they all come in to this harbor and lay all night.

June 13 This day on board ship *Ann*. Sailed schooner *Lee*, Waters, and returned by noon. Came from Eastward D. Chapman with the Reverend Mr. Weeks and his family and the widow Hannah Dixey.

June 14 This day at noon Quilty, Antiton, and myself are discharged from ship *Ann*. This afternoon the ship came in to Colonel Lee's wharf. The Yankees obliged Commodore Banks to quit his post and sailed for Halifax with 12 sail of shipping with him. All our cruisers out.

June 15 This day the inhabitants are unloading ship *Ann* at Colonel Lee['s wharf]. Anchored schooner *Franklin*, [John] Skimmer, and sailed again. A ship and brig off. All our cruisers out.

June 16 This morning five of the Continental cruiser are attacking the ship and brig. Cannon fired all day. This evening 7 sail of cruiser attacked the ship and brig. A constant firing of cannon till 12 at night.

The ship and brig are taken. Preaching at St. Michael's, and the 2 houses. Sailed Will Andrews for Spain.

June 17 This day fair, Wind SW. A ship off. Tis said four men are killed on board our privateers and a major of the Regulars. A Town Meeting about Independency and throwed off King George the 3, as tis said.

6. Campaign in the Middle Colonies (1776–77)

[These short entries express much of the uncertainty and misinformation that circulated through New England during the Revolutionary War. The entry for 6 January 1777 refers to the Battle of Trenton. Source: Smith, ed., *Journals of Ashley Bowen*, 45: 503, 504, 505, 509, 511.]

Nov. 22 This day at Boston. Tis said that Fort Washington is taken by the British troops.[1]

* * * * *

Nov. 28 This day came in the *True Blue* cruiser, Captain William Coles, commander. Sailed sloop *Rover*, Abijah Boden, commander. Tis said the King's troops are in possession of all the forts in New York Government. Sailed LeCraw.

* * * * *

Dec. 11 This day cold. Several schooners came up with wood. Many prisoners are in town for to go in the flag of truce. Tis said there hath been a battle and that eight thousand of the European troops are killed and taken.[2]

Dec. 13 Close smoky weather. I heard a man that rides post say that there hath been no battle as yet and that General Howe is within 30 miles of Philadelphia with his army of 18 thousand men, and marches on his own ground right out.

* * * * *

---

1 Fort Washington along with 3,000 American soldiers had, indeed, surrendered to the British on 16 November.

2 Unfounded rumor.

Jan. 6 This day cold. I went to farm. Handbills about taking the Hessians &c.[1] Died suddenly Mr. Stone at the farm.

* * * * *

Feb. 8 This day much rain. Wind southerly. Tis said that there hath been lately terrible times in [New] Jersey but no handbills out. I dined at Captain Prince's farm.

7. Religion and Revolution in Marblehead

[See also the poem "On Revolution and Religion" (Appendix E1b). St. Michael's Church was the Anglican church in Marblehead. "Dry Bones" and "Salt Peters" refer to the two Congregationalist churches in Marblehead. The First Church met in the Old Meeting House; the Second Church met in the New Meeting House. Source: Smith, ed., *Journals of Ashley Bowen*, 45: 497, 505, 511, 515, 549, 550.]

Aug. 1, 1776 This day a Provincial Fast. Preaching at St. Michael's Church and Dry Bones. No preaching at Salt Peter's. Whitwell attending wife at Boston with smallpox. Sailed O'Brien on a cruise. Sailed O'Burke to Boston for repair.

* * * * *

Dec. 12 Yankee feast. Some snow. Passed a brig for Beverly. Prayer and a sermon at St. Michael's and something at the two public houses. Tis said that Whitwell and Story gave their God their thanks for the bare-feeted army's having killed six thousands and taken two thousands of the British army prisoners.[2] Tis the easiest thing in the world to be mistaken as well in the High Pit as the Low Pit.

* * * * *

Feb. 9, 1777 This day fair weather, but the streets are very slippery. The New Laws hath shut up St. Michael's Church. The Will of God be

---

1 This refers to the American Victory at Trenton on 26 December.

2 William Whitwell and Isaac Story were the ministers of the First and Second Congregational Churches in Marblehead.

done, but I hope it will be opened again before this year is out. St. Michael's Church shut up by the laws of the land. So much for Fort Washington being taken by the Britons! Marblehead February 1777—Parson Weeks a prisoner at home &c.

* * * * *

Feb. 16 Fair and Pleasant, but no flags out at Fort nor preaching at St. Michael's. Oh Lord have Mercy on us miserable creatures; the worst is to come!

* * * * *

Mar. 28 This day is, according to the canons of the Church of England, called Good Friday, but the Church of St. Michael's being in bondage by the men of Liberty we had no prayers or preaching.

* * * * *

Feb. 1, 1780 A meeting at St. Michael's Church and voted that it shall be opened and Mr. Woodward Abraham appointed to read prayers and sermons, nothing to be done contrary to the laws of the land. Thomas Porter chose Church Clerk. This day smart cold. All the Proprietors of St. Michael's Church met and concluded to open it on Sunday next.

* * * * *

Feb. 6 This day smart cold. We have St. Michael's Church opened again. Mr. Woodward Abraham read prayers and a sermon. Mr. Porter, Clerk. This day St. Michael's Church was opened, and I was very happy to have prayer again in the best manner that we could, agreeable to the times &c.

Appendix E: Personal Writings of Ashley Bowen

1. Poetry

[These poems are scattered throughout Bowen's different journals and notebooks. *On Smallpox* and *On Revolution and Religion* are clearly of Bowen's own invention; *On Marriage* is probably a sailor's song, which Bowen may have heard and copied down, because it appealed to him. Source: Smith, ed., *Journals of Ashley Bowen*, 45: 343–44, 522–23, 594–95.]

a. On Smallpox

A sore distemper is crept in
It seized on all both old and young
But by what means I cannot tell
And very fatal proves to some.

In Scripture we may plainly see
And read such words as these
Can evil in the city be
Except the Lord be pleased.

Short-sighted creatures as we are
Could not our danger see
Tho often-times distressed with fear
What this disease should be.

Surely the hand of Providence
Over us did bear a sway
Tho we so much distressed with fear
Must fall an easy prey.

The 24 day of July
We were all fenced around
Before the 17 of August came
Eight bodies are lain in the ground.

How do you think dear friends
What we must feel within
To see so many carried out
That had our neighbors been.

Not only neighbors unto some
But their dear friends likewise
Which makes our very hearts relent
And draws tears from our eyes.

Let's not impute it all to chance
Nor merely second cause
But let us view the hand of God
As what we do deserve.

b. On Revolution and Religion

As for opinions, I confess
I never upon them laid stress
Sometimes a Whig, sometimes a Tory
But seldom steadfast in one story.
The reason is, I'm not yet fixed
So my religion is but mixed.
Yet, most of all, I do incline
The Old Episcopalian line;
Yet not so fixed on this head,
But I can turn my coat for bread,
Yet don't mistake my meaning, as
If from the truth I meant to pass;
The essential parts of my opinion
Is not in any sect's dominion
Nor will I e'er be tied to think
That in one spring I ought to drink
In Christendom we all affect:
The Christian name in some respect:
Yet to our shame and our derision
We're full of schisms and divisions
Some are Papists, some are Prelates
Some are Quakers and some Zealots
Some Anabaptists, some Aquarians

Some Antinomians, and some Arians:
Some are Free Willers and some Ranters:
Some Presbyterian covenanters;
Some Erskinites to gain probation:
Some Glasites, some for presentation[1]
Though these all aim at heaven at last,
Their diff'rence puts me in a gast;
To follow which I cannot tell,
Therefore I bid them all farewell;
Because I knew, that faith and love
The sphere is wherein I should move
For sure without true Charity
None can enjoy Felicity
But Charity, now at this day,
She is obliged to fly away,
Instead of which envy and hate
Contempt, resentment, and debate,
Is most in each society,
This makes me all these sects deny
Tis not in word as I do read
But Christians, must be so in-deed;
So Madam, this is all my creed,
Marblehead August the 1 1776
A Provincial Fast Day &c &c
We have more Thursday Fasts than God

c. On Marriage

As you mean to set sail
For the Land of Delight
And in Wedlock's soft hammock
To swing every night
If you hope that your
Voyage successful shall prove

1 Anabaptists, Aquarians, Antinomians, Arians, Free Willers, Ranters, Presbyterian Covenanters, Erskinites, and Glasites were all different branches of Protestant belief. That Bowen even knew about them, some of which had few if any American adherents, is a testimony either to his own religious knowledge or to the degree to which the particulars of faith were topics of interest within Marblehead's maritime society.

Fill your sails with affection
Your cabin with love.
Fill your sails with affection &c. *Chorus*

Let your heart like the mainmast
Be ever up-right
And the Union you boast like
Our tackle be tight
Of the shoals of indifference be
Sure to keep clear
And the quicksands of jealousy
Never come near.

Chorus
And the quicksands &c.

If husbands e'er hope to live peaceable lives
They must reckon themselves give
The helm to their
Wives
For the evener we go Boys the better
We sail
And on ship-board the helm is
Still ruled by the tail.

Chorus
And on ship-board the helm &c.

Then list to your pilot my Boys
And be wise
If my precepts you
Scorn and my maxims despise
A brace of proud antlers
Your brows may adorn
And a hundred to one but you'll
Double Cape Horn[1]

---

1 To double Cape Horn is to round Cape Horn. Bowen is suggesting here that those who ignore his advice are likely not only to be cuckolded, but to spend their lives in as much misery as sailors experience voyaging around Cape Horn.

2. Dreams

[As the story of the courtship of Dorothy Chadwick proves clearly, Bowen believed in the portentous character of dreams. These are only the most elaborate of the many mentioned in his writings. Source: Smith, ed., *Journals of Ashley Bowen*, 45: 606, 607–08.]

Nov. 22, 1796

In the night I dreamed I was standing by Doctor Story, I supposed about 11 o'clock, and I thought of dinner and suppose that I had a quarter of lamb at the old mansion house,[1] and I went round the Town House, and I found a fore-quarter of lamb in my hand, and right in the center between T[own] House Captain Gordon. I saw a large hole and Mother Mary Bowen[2] sat on the right hand. Mother Bowen gave me a key of a padlock which she gave me to unlock a cupboard door and there appeared a live mouse, and I brushed it off in the water and then the lock was full of dead mice, and I cleared it out and unlocked the lock and nothing in it, so I took my fore-quarter and came home.

Sept. 23, 1804

This morning at 2 o'clock A.M. as I lay sick of a fever, my wife laying by me, I supposed that I was spoke to or beckoned to by a hand to follow it, and I passed Nova Scotia and that part of North America and the Atlantic Sea as far as the Channel of England as far as the South Foreland in England where I supposed that I was landed at. And as I descended to the seashore I saw some men by the shore-side. It seemed the last quarter of the Moon and very heavy clouds, a small dim light of fire &c. I saw two men on my right hand, and as they talked one said, "What must I do, for I cannot let him go! I shall be hanged by 11 o'clock!" As the two men were talking I said to the other men, "Gentlemen! Do you know one Bowen in the British naval service?"[3] which they said that they did

1 Dr. Story was Isaac Story the minister of the Second Congregational Church in Marblehead. The old mansion house was the house in which Ashley grew up. It still stands, across the street from the Town House.

2 Mother Mary Bowen was Ashley's second stepmother. His first stepmother, Hannah Harris Bowen, had died in 1764, and his father remarried the same year Mary Russell Boden, the "Mother Mary" referred to here. She died in 1838.

3 Who this Bowen is remains unclear, unless Ashley is in some supernatural way observing himself.

and said that he belonged to that ship and showed me a ship, it being thick and dark. I said could I get a-put off to her? I asked what this Bowen was on board, and they said Master and Commander of her, and as I stood one of them said, "That is the man that is now talking with the other." And directly Mr. Bowen left the other man and came to me and said, "How do you do, Sir?" And I asked him how he could send for me as I was very sick at home. He said, "Sir, you were always good to direct me when I was in distress, and I am in great distress now for I have received a commission from King George the Third to burn, sink, and destroy all French Republicans and more especially that usurper Bonaparte himself," and one said that that was the man. Now there was a man stood by himself, being well dressed. Bowen said, "If I should let him go I should be hanged by 11 o'clock at the Admiral's yard arm," and I said, "Let me see your Commission." And I took it to the small light and saw that it was according as Mr. Bowen reported. And I asked the men if they would help Mr. Bowen. They said, "Sir, if you are acquainted in the Navy you must know that we must obey our superior officer," and said that he, the Third Officer, wished to have nothing to do with the said Bonaparte, and they would not assist him, so I supposed it to be a treacherous trick, and in order to save Mr. Bowen's life, I having the Commission in my hand, I went to this man said to be Bonaparte and took him by the arm and said, "Sir, by virtue of Mr. Bowen's Commission you are my prisoner!" He shew me a small roll of paper and said it was a number of bills on France, payable on sight, and shew me a purse of guineas, and I said I would have nothing to do with either of them. And I took a handkerchief and pinned his arms and asked the seamen to assist me, but they would not, and I took Bonaparte by his left arm and Lieutenant Bowen on my left hand and we went up the hill. And when we came to Dover Castle they would not receive us, and then we set out for the Tower of London, and the other officers and men followed us at a small distance, and when we arrived at the bridge we saw no more of them and we came over the bridge. We came to the Tower where we got a receipt for Mr. Bonaparte, and we returned to the South Foreland, and I came home the same track as I went, and I found my wife and the body as I left it, and as soon as I come to myself I heard the clock strike 4. My wife said, "You have lain quiet some time!"

Appendix F: Contemporary Accounts of Marblehead

1. Reverend John Barnard (1714-66)

[John Barnard was the pastor of the First Congregational Church in Marblehead from 1714 to 1770. Towards the end of his life, Barnard composed a lengthy autobiography, and in it he devoted these pages to the development of Marblehead as a seaport. Source: John Barnard, "Autobiography of the Reverend John Barnard, Nov. 14, 1766," Massachusetts Historical Society, *Collections*, 3rd Ser., 5 (1836): 240.]

Suffer me to turn aside, and take a view of the very different state of the town, upon worldly accounts, since I came into it. When I first came, [in 1714] there were two companies of poor, smoke-dried, rude, ill-clothed men, trained to no military discipline but that of "*whipping the snake*," as they called it; whereas now, [in 1766] and for years past, we are a distinct regiment, consisting of seven full companies, well clad, of bright countenances, vigorous and active men, so well trained in the use of their arms, and the various motions and marches, that I have heard some Colonels of other regiments, and a Brigadier General say, they never saw throughout the country, not in their own regiment, no, nor in Boston, so goodly an appearance of spirited men, and so well exercised a regiment. When I came, there was not so much as one proper carpenter, nor mason, nor tailor, nor butcher in the town, nor any thing of a market worth naming; but they had their houses built by country workmen, and their clothes made out of town, and supplied themselves with beef and pork from Boston, which drained the town of its money. But now we abound in artificers, and some of the best, and our markets large, even to a full supply. And, what above all I would remark, there was not so much as one foreign trading vessel belonging to the town, nor for several years after I came into it; though no town had really greater advantages in their hands. The people contented themselves to be the slaves that digged in the mines, and left the merchants of Boston, Salem, and Europe, to carry away the gains; by which means the town was always in dismally poor circumstances, involved in debt to the merchants more than they were worth; nor could I find twenty families in it that, upon the best examination, could stand upon their own legs; and they were generally as rude, swearing, drunken, and fighting a crew, as they were poor. Whereas, not only are the public ways vastly mended, but the manners of the people greatly cultivated; and we have many gentlemanlike and polite families, and the very fishermen generally scorn the rudenesses of the former generation.

I soon saw that the town had a price in its hands, and it was a pity they had not a heart to improve it. I therefore laid myself out to get acquaintance with the English masters of vessels, that I might by them be let into the mystery of the fish trade, and in a little time I gained a pretty thorough understanding in it. When I saw the advantages of it, I thought it my duty to stir up my people, such as I thought, would hearken to me, and were capable of practising upon the advice, to send the fish to market themselves, that they might reap the benefit of it, to the enriching themselves, and serving the town. But, alas! I could inspire no man with courage and resolution enough to engage in it, till I met with Mr. Joseph Swett, a young man of strict justice, great industry, enterprising genius, quick apprehension, and firm resolution, but of small fortune.[1] To him I opened myself fully, laid the scheme clearly before him, and he hearkened unto me, and was wise enough to put it in practice. He first sent a small cargo to Barbadoes. He soon found he increased his stock, built vessels, and sent the fish to Europe, and prospered in the trade, to the enriching of himself; and some of his family, by carrying on the trade, have arrived at large estates. The more promising young men of the town soon followed his example; that now we have between thirty and forty ships, brigs, snows, and topsail schooners engaged in foreign trade. From so small a beginning the town has risen into its present flourishing circumstances, and we need no foreigner to transport our fish, but are able ourselves to send it all to the market. Let God have the praise, who has redeemed the town from a state of bondage into a state of liberty and freedom.

---

1 Joseph Swett (1689–1776) became one of Marblehead's first locally resident merchants involved primarily in foreign trade (and not just the outfitting of fishing schooners). His daughter, Martha, married Jeremiah Lee, the wealthiest merchant that colonial Massachusetts ever produced.

2. Alexander Hamilton (1744)

[This particular Alexander Hamilton was a Scottish physician who settled in Annapolis, Maryland, in 1739. In 1744 he traveled north on a tour of the colonies and passed through most of the larger towns and cities of the Atlantic seaboard ending up in York on the coast of Maine. For the most part, Hamilton mixed with the local intelligentsia—lawyers, ministers, and other physicians—yet he was a keen observer of the physical layout of these towns as well as the business they conducted. The journal of his travels includes the following account of his visit to Marblehead, which among other things gives a short description of St. Michael's—Bowen's own church. Source: Alexander Hamilton, *Gentleman's Progress: The Itinerarium of Dr. Alexander Hamilton, 1744*, ed., Carl Bridenbaugh (Chapel Hill, NC: U of North Carolina P, 1948): 118–19.]

July 28 Att one o'clock I arrived att Marblehead, a large fishing town, lying upon the sea coast, built upon a rock and standing pritty bleak to the easterly winds from the sea. It lyes 18 miles N.E. from Boston and is somewhat larger than Albany but not so neatly or compactly built, the houses being all of wood, and the streets very uneven, narrow, and irregular. It contains about 5000 inhabitants, and their commodity is fish. There is round the town above 200 acres of land covered with fish flakes,[1] upon which they dry their cod. There are 90 fishing sloops always employed, and they deal for 34,000£ sterling prime cost value in fish yearly, bringing in 30,000 quintalls, a quintall being 100 weight dryed fish, which is 3,000,000 pound weight, a great quantity of that commodity.

I put up here att one Reid's att the Sign of the Dragon, and while I was att dinner, Mr. Malcolm, the Church of England minister to whom I was recommended, came in. After I had dined he carried me round the town and showed me the fish flakes and the town battery, which is built upon a rock, naturally well fortified, and mounts about 12 large guns. We had a great deal of talk about affairs at home. I went to his house and drank tea with him. He showed me some pritty pieces of musick and played some tunes on the flute and violin. He is author of a very good book upon musick which shows his judgement and knowledge in that part of science.

---

1 Fish flakes were the rough tables on which salt cod was set out to dry.

Sunday, July 29 This morning enquiring for my portmanteau, I was told by my man Dromo that it was in his room. I had the curiosity to go and see what kind of a room his room was and, upon a reconoitre, found it a most spacious one, furnished alamode de cabaret with tables, chairs, a fine feather bed with quilted counterpine, white callicoe canopy or tester, and curtains, every way adapted for a gentleman of his degree and complexion.

I went to church to hear Mr. Malcolim in the forenoon, who gave us a pritty discourse. This church is a building of wood about 80 foot square, supported in the inside with eight large octagonal wooden pillars of the Dorick order. Upon this church stands a steeple in which there is a publick clock. The floor of the church is raised 6 or 7 foot above the ground, and under it is a burying place. The pulpit and altar are neat enough, the first being set out with a cushion of red velvet, and the other painted and adorned with the King's arms at top. There is one large gallery facing the pulpit, opposite to which at the south entry of the church hangs a pritty large gilt candle branch. The congregation consisted of about 400 people. I dined with Mr. Malcolm and went to church again with him in the afternoon and spent the evening agreeably in his company. In this town are likewise two great Presbyterian meetings.[1]

3. Francis Goelet (1750)

[Francis Goelet was a New York merchant and shipowner with business all around the North Atlantic. In 1750 he embarked on a voyage to London and stopped off briefly in his passage to visit eastern Massachusetts. While in Boston, he spent several days touring the North Shore and made the following observations on the town of Marblehead. Source: Francis Goelet, *The Voyages and Travels of Francis Goelet, 1746–1758*, ed. Kenneth Scott (Flushing, NY: Queens College P, 1970), entry for October 21, 1750.]

1750 October 21st Salem Wee arrived at Marblehead about 10 a clock, which is about 4 miles by land, trough a pleasent country and good roades, and is about 1½ miles by water. It forms a bay. Marblehead lays on the eastermost part the land but the west side the bay, and Salem on a point, the westermost part the land & eastermost side the bay. Before

---

1 Presbyterian meetings refer to the two Congregationalist churches.

you enter Marblehead, the roads are excessive stoney & land very rockey, affording only very little pasture ground. Put up at Mr. Read's where breakfast, & then went to see the towne of Marblehead. Has about 450 houses, all wood & clapboarded, the generallity miserable buildings, mostly close in with the rocks, with rockey foundations, very cragy & crasey. The whole towne is built upon a rock, which is heigh & steep to the water. The harbour is shelterd by an island, which runs along parralell to it and brakes of the sea. Vessells may ride heere very safe. There is a path or way downe to the warf, which is but small & on which is a large ware house, where they land their fish &c. From this heigh, cliffty shore it took its name. I saw about 5 topsail vessells & about 40 schooners & sloops in the harbour. They had then about 70 sail schooners a fishing, with about 600 men & boys imployd in the fishery. They take vast quantitys cod, which they cure heere. Saw several thousand flakes then cureing. This place is noted for children and noureeches the most of any place for its bigness in North America. It's said the chief cause is attributed to their feeding on cods' heads &c., which is their prin[c]ipall diet. The greatest distaste a person has to this place is the stench of the fish. The whole air seems tainted with it. It may, in short, be said it's a dirty, erregular, stincking place.

4. Ensign Francis Williams (1775)

[Francis Williams was an ensign in the Continental army at the outset of the Revolutionary War. Although his description of Marblehead is even grimmer than Goelet's, it should be remembered that Williams passed through Marblehead after the outbreak of the war, when the fishery had been shut down, and most local families were finding it nearly impossible to make ends meet. Source: "Ensign Williams' Visit to Essex County in 1776," Essex Institute, *Historical Collections*, 83 (1947): 144–45.]

We pass'd on over a Stony Road to Marblehead, which is a dirty disagreeable Place at present they are here in great Distress as the Town is built amongst Rocks & Stones, where is no land to cultivate

Marblehead and the people in general are Fishermen or concer'd in that Way, which Source of Support is now at an end many of the men are in the army & the Rest are out of Employ and almost every house swarms with Children of these hardy, temporate Men—

Their situation is miserable the Streets & Roads are fill'd the poor little Boys & Girls who are forc'd beg of all they see the Women are lazy & of Consequence dirty Creatures—there are about 400 houses here & 4 or 5 of them large neat houses—they have a small Battery in a Point near to try to keep of the men of War

One remarkable object of Charity here was a little Boy whose left arm was shriveled up & dead and his Legs were contracted and folded up like a Taylors, and of no strength this emaciated creature would move in an odd manner with the assistance of his Right hand into the middle of the Road before your horse and would beg in a most moving manner and you must give him something or drive over him—I do not want ever to see such another Place—

5. Robert Honyman (1775)

[Robert Honyman was a Scottish physician who settled in Virginia in 1772 and decided to tour the northern colonies in 1775. He visited Marblehead on an outing from Boston late in March. Source: Robert Honyman, *Colonial Panorama, 1775: Dr. Robert Honyman's Journal for March and April* ed., Peter Padelford (San Marino, CA: Huntington Library, 1939): 47–48.]

Mar. 23 About 6 set off for Marble head, which is 4 miles from Salem, & the Steeples of Marble head may be seen from Salem. The road is pretty good, considering the rocky country it passes through, almost entirely bare of earth, & yet here along the road are many good houses. Past over a bridge at the head of a branch of the road of Salem which runs up a long way to the Southward of the Town. Arrived at Marbel head about dark; went to a Tavern, got supper, & sate talking with company till 10 & then went to bed.

Mar. 24 Rose between 6 & 7 this morning, & notwithstanding it snowed & was extremely cold walked all over the town & examined it. Marble head is reckoned to contain more people than Salem, contains a number of fine houses, though it is extremely irregular, the Houses being built on the Top, on the sides, & at the bottom of rocks, wherever they could find a convenient situation. The harbour is very spacious, being open to the Sea at the East end, & having some Islands lying without which secures it in some measure from the Sea. I believe it is joined to the road of Salem. The Harbour is formed by a large arm of the Sea running in South west between the main & a neck of Land which lyes opposite to the town & runs Eastward till it reaches the mouth of the Harbour. It is properly a Bay or road, where the Vessels ly at anchor, & there are wharfs before the town where the Vessels come to load & unload. Before the town on the rocks are numberless Stages for drying Fish, & the same at Salem. The trade of Marble head is the same as at Salem cheifly cod, Oil & west India trade, but it is not reckoned to have so much trade as Salem. They send the best of their Fish up the Straits, & the rest to the West Indies.[1] The best fish they catch in the winter & early in the spring, & these sometimes sells for a Guinea the Quintal, or 112 Pounds; the others in common sell for about 10 or 11 Shillings Sterling. I counted the Vessels here & there were about 60 or 70, almost all of them Schooners & sloops. The Lively man of war of 20 Guns lyes here at present.—Marble head is famous for the number of children born & brought up here. They have rope walks here as at Salem of great length.—

6. Francisco de Miranda (1784)

[Francisco de Miranda was born in Venezuela in 1750. As a young man, he had purchased himself a commission in the Spanish army but was arrested for embezzlement in 1782 and being convicted by a Spanish court fled to America, where he began a lifelong campaign to agitate for the liberation of the Spanish New World colonies. This entry, part of a diary he seems to have kept through much of his adult life, describes the state of Marblehead after the conclusion of the Revolutionary War. Source: Francisco de Miranda, *The New Democracy: Travels of Francisco de Miranda in the United States, 1783–84*, ed. John S Ezell (Norman, Oklahoma, 1963): 188–89.]

Sept. 27 Around eleven o'clock Mr. Wetmore and I sallied forth in a chaise to Marblehead, four miles distant. The road is very good until one is about to enter this town of fishermen, which is completely surrounded by rocks; upon these the houses are built. The appearance of the place indicates perfectly what it is. The houses are poor, but filled with people, particularly children, whose number is proportionately

---

1 The phrase, "up the Straits," means past Gibraltar and into the Mediterranean. Most Marblehead fish was exported to Spain.

larger than in any other town I have seen (Mr. Wetmore and I counted five hundred boys playing in the street); nevertheless all are suitably dressed, which shows there is no need at home. As we went down to the shore on the stony and uneven streets, we saw on all sides a multitude of stretchers filled with drying fish (not a small addition to the fishing scene said town represents); likewise a fort built at the entrance of the small bridge there, where the ships take shelter. Presently we returned to Salem, observing for the second time the number of boys in the streets. The women have the reputation of scandalous customs, and it is said around there that Marblehead is remarkable for the many children and people of red hair. In the last war it suffered immensely, but since the peace, recovers its prosperity with great progress. There are two conspicuous buildings in this town besides the church; these are the houses of Colonel Lee and Mr. Hooper, very clear proof that the poor always have to make somebody rich.

Houses	600
Inhabitants	6,000
Fishing vessels, which catch yearly 60,000 hundred-weights of codfish	60

7. George Washington (1789)

[George Washington made a triumphal tour of New England in the fall of 1789, soon after assuming the presidency of the United States. He passed through Marblehead on his way northward and in his diary confirmed some of the sentiments expressed by other visitors earlier in the century. Source: George Washington, *The Diaries of George Washington*, 6 vols., ed. Donald Jackson (Charlottesville, VA: UP of Virginia, 1976–79), 5: 483.]

The Chief employmt. of the People of Marblehead (Males) is fishing—about 110 Vessels and 800 Men and boys are engaged in this business. Their chief export is fish. About 5000 Souls are said to be in this place which has the appearance of antiquity. The Houses are old—the streets dirty—and the common people not very clean. Before we entered the Town we were met, & attended by a Comee. till we were handed over to the Select Men who conducted us saluted by artily. in to the Town—to the House of a Mrs. Lee where there was a cold Collation prepared—after partaking of which we visited the Harbour—their fish brakes for curing fish—&ca. and then proceeded (first receiving an Address from the Inhabitants) to Salem.

Appendix G: Miscellaneous Writings

1. Journal of Elizabeth Bowen Martin

[Elizabeth Bowen was Ashley's younger sister by six years, meaning that she was only five when their mother died. Though her description of her mother's religious beliefs must be taken with a grain of salt, she knew her father well and seems to have agreed with Ashley that he was a somewhat cold and distant character. Source: *Elizabeth Bowen, Diary, 1775–1808*, Bowen Family Papers, James Duncan Phillips Library, Peabody-Essex Museum, Salem, Mass., cited in Smith, ed., *Journals of Ashley Bowen*, 44: 8n.]

There was Nine of us Left without a tender guide & the advantage of a Religious Education … But my father marring his second wife It seemd with him as with most men to be too much taken up with the things of this world to the neglect of there Children and familys. My father being of the Baptits perswasion would not have his Children Baptized in their Infancy which was a great grief to my mother who was perswaded of their obligations to it as a Christian duty, we were all capable & forward to Receive Instructions but my mother being dead and my father taken up with the things of this world...did not take that care of our education.

2. Letter from Nathan Bowen to Ashley Bowen (24 May 1757)

[This formal letter is suggestive of the relationship that existed between Ashley and his father. Source: Marblehead Historical Society, cited in Smith, ed., *Journals of Ashley Bowen* 1: 44n.]

My Son

If this Should reach you let it Serve to Acquaint you that the family are Well except yr Mother, who remains in the State you left her in. I simpathize with you under your late Misfortune with Capt. Lewis, but hope you will retreive that loss by a due Improvement of the Oppertunities you now have, let me recommend you to a Steady Honest & Honourable pursuit of the Things of this World, I Shall rejoice to hear from you of your health, but gladder to See you when it will Suit you to return to Marblehead, always behaving in Such a Manner as Shall recommend you to the favour of God & man, I heartily wish you health and am your Effectionate father.

Nathan Bowen

3. From the *Boston News-Letter and New England Chronicle* (10 March 1763)

[This is an interesting episode that occurred on the Boston waterfront and was recorded in the local newspaper but only alluded to in Bowen's autobiography as the voyage of the *Rambler* to Boston (p. 77). It may go some way to explaining why it was that his career as a ship's officer was never particularly successful.]

Morning about 1 o'Clock, a small schooner from Marblehead, Bowen, Master, overset at the Long Wharf, and fill's with Water; and had it not been for the Assistance of some of the Town Watchmen the People on board would have been drowned.

4. From a Letter from Ashley Bowen to the Reverend William Bentley (14 May 1807)

[The following passage, contained in a letter to Bowen's friend William Bentley, is in spite of its rambling nature the closest thing to a statement of political philosophy that Bowen ever wrote. Source: Smith, ed., *Journals of Ashley Bowen* 45: 615–16.]

But My Friend Excuse me while I remark on something Extra ie the Friendship & good understanding that now Subsists between you & myself or rather your bounty & good will towards me for Several reasons the remark is Pertinent 1st I am a poor man & you are Rich. 2d our Political oppinions are as opposite as the Poles ... when I hear So much Said About *Patriotism* & *Republickism* the latter I Profess not to understand—look at france is this it—as to the former I Consider myself Second to no man be his Professions what they may I appeal to my Papers & Journals & Submit them to the Candid world they will live in the Panthion of fame tho like Columbus & Bellisarius I die Poor & Obscure—Sir Call to view 6th of April [17]59. the drums going about Town beating up forVolunteers—to go & take Quebeck. the 19th of april 75[1] is recent in our minds but as the other war Prior it had more of Novelty & Sublemity—our Country was alive & Marblehead—like Marblehead—was all fire—King & Country was the theme & the order of the day the drums began in the Morn and the Voice of the People was—heve a go heve a go only give us a head to lead us Judge of my feeling on this occasion. King & Country at stake—& the People only calling for a Leader by noon I could no longer resist. I said I will take the Charge Ashley Bowen—Ashley Bowen hath consented to lead us—*Viva La Rex Viva La Rex* was the Cry thro the Day which was Concluded with festivitys & the Early dawn of the Succeeding day—was witness to our Zeal—& our march to head Quotters.

Sir this was not a Momentary Flash—to Pass off like the Early dens here was our all at Stake & our lives offerd—the impression is indeliable nothing pecuniary was expected or calculated upon but to Preserve or retrieve our Countrys Honor—my own & the Publick records will prove the fact and the Sequel—& my reward hath been *what*—why I have had the approbation of the King & the candid & the *magnanimous* at this day do me Honour for my Zeal & fidellity (this is Consolatory I must Confess)—I have no reason to repine neither Shall I be ungratefull my Country hath not been—the Unfortunate Seventy five[2] made a Sgnn that deranged all the Plans of the most able Statesmen for years on the subject—the allwise knows his own Purposes I must have patience and hope traach on—& I am so much of a peedertinarian[3] that I feel Perswaded I shall have that I am to have being now in the Vicinity of Four Score why shall I be anxious ...

5. From William Bentley's Diary

[William Bentley was from 1783–1819 the minister of the Second Congregational (East) Church located in Salem's maritime ward. A republican in politics, a friend of the French Revolution, and a Unitarian in his religious leanings, he is best known as the author of a remarkable diary, covering almost his entire pastorate and recounting in rich detail the local history of Salem during those years. Traveling around the region and talking with people such as Bowen was one of his favorite hobbies. Bentley erred both on Bowen's

1 The date of the Battles of Lexington and Concord.

2 Another reference to the outbreak of the American Revolution.

3 Bowen meant predestinarian.

birthdate (1728) and the year of the Quebec expedition (1759). Source: William Bentley, *The Diary of William Bentley, D.D.*, 4 vols. (Salem, MA: The Essex Institute, 1911), 3:124–25.]

Nov. 30, 1804 This day I went to Marblehead to dine with Capt. J. Prince. I was received with great hospitality & had the company of Capt. Nathan Martin at dinner. After dinner we were entertained by the original manner of Capt. Ashley Bowen, aged 78, born in 1726.[1] In 1749, he took command of 32 men from Marblehead, who entered into the marine service, & they were transported to Halifax. There he found Admiral Durell & entered as a Midshipman on board the Pembroke of 50 guns under Capt. Simcoe, who died on the passage & was succeeded by Capt. Wheelock of the Squirrel Frigate of 20 guns. He was with James Cook, sailing master of the Pembroke, in the survey of the St. Lawrence as his documents shew. This same Cook is the immortal Circumnavigator. Mr. Ashley Bowen's claims are real but how far they extend to the whole work, could be learnt only by seeing what Cook has given to the public. Mr. Bowen has proofs from his papers of being in that survey with James Cook. I was much pleased with the strength of memory, original manners, & facetious discourse of this old sailor, who pleads warmly for a pension as he is now, as he expressed it, under "bare poles." A curious representation of his own life under the figure of a Ship, had much fancy, & pleasing expression. I was highly disposed to give him every assistance in gaining public relief.

* * * * *

Feb 4, 1813 Was at Marblehead at the funeral of Capt. Ashley Bowen my old friend. He fell sometime since from a deck & was injuried. Lately on a step & was confined. He died after a short illness, probably from a mortification. The same firm man. With all his prejudices & with sacred attachment to British everything, Navy, Church, State, so much did he love the memory of 1759 & his intimate friendship with Cooke the Circumnavigator. I had the consent of the Capt. at the Fort for the troops in procession, but the wife refused. The Cong. minister prayed at the house & the Eng. Ep. at the Grave. He was interred in a spot chosen by himself in the New M.H. ground, with his kindred, but so as to rise & face St. Michael's Church. He was a man of as fine stamina

---

1 Bowen was born in 1728 and was 76 at this time.

of life as I ever knew. His understanding quick, his pursuit eager, resolute & inexhaustible. His probity sure & undisguised. His friendship sovereign & eternal. My father was with him among the Carpenters of 1759, when he was among the seamen. Mr. Bowen had his journals, his plans, his notices of all occurrences, but he was as completely [in]formed upon the Quebec expedition as the human mind can admit & his last thought as powerful as his first.

6. Ashley Bowen's Obituary, *Essex Register*, Salem (6 February 1813)

[This obituary was almost certainly composed by William Bentley.]

Died at Marblehead on Tuesday last [2 February 1813], Capt. ASHLEY BOWEN, aged 86.[1] This extraordinary man was born in 1728, and by power of intellect, soul of purpose, and unity of character, was distinguished through life. All his faculties lived with him till he expired, and they all took their leave of him together. Before his death he suffered by a fall, as he had once before in his active life, and these proved the cause of his death, almost without the form of disease, and without any interruption of that firmness which never forsook him. In the war in Canada he was known as the best man to unite authority, with a sure influence on the seamen who were drawn out to attend the expedition in 1759, and he had every testimony of full success. When he had reached Quebec he found a soul congenial with his own, the immortal circumnavigator Cooke, and with him he surveyed the river, and every thing which could exercise their talent, and could prove useful to the expedition. The Great Cooke continued in the career upon which he gloriously entered, and has the ample record of his fame. The scene of Mr. Bowen's life was different from that of his ambition. With his New England friends he returned, and by their sympathies was directed to the employments of his home. But not a trace was ever lost of the former scene, nor could he change in the slightest degree the form of thought which his mind had taken, when he left the St. Lawrence. All his views of Marine Greatness were from the omnipotence of the British navy, and tho' his country was dear to him, he never could perceive the path through which she could move to marine power. This state of mind arose from the contemplation through a long life of only one object that filled his soul. Had he begun his career at the present moment, we have

1 Bowen was 85 when he died.

no doubt from him we might have dated glory to our country. The probity of this extraordinary man has always been admired. His journals and papers have proved his attention to every thing which passed before him, and his constitution of mind did not suffer the least apparent change till his dissolution. Time must turn over many a page, and review many a record, before he points to such another man.

Select Bibliography

Contemporary Mariners' Narratives

Cremer, John. *Ramblin' Jack: The Journal of Captain John Cremer, 1700–1774*, ed. R. Reynell Bellamy. London: J. Cape, 1936.

Kelly, Samuel. *Samuel Kelly: An Eighteenth Century Seaman*, ed. Crosbie Garstin. New York: Frederick A. Stokes, 1925.

The Nagle Journal: a Diary of the Life of Jacob Nagle, Sailor, From the Year 1775 to 1841, ed., John C. Dann. New York: Weidenfeld & Nicolson, 1988.

Prince, Christopher. *The Autobiography of a Yankee Mariner: Christopher Prince and the American Revolution*, ed. Michael J. Crawford. Washington, DC: Brassey's 2002.

Secondary Sources

Bolster, W. Jeffrey. *Black Jacks: African American Seamen in the Age of Sail*. Cambridge, MA: Harvard UP, 1997.

Crane, Elaine Forman. *Ebb Tide in New England: Women, Seaports, and Social Change, 1630–1800*. Boston: Northeastern UP, 1998.

Creighton, Margaret S. *Rites and Passages: The Experience of American Whaling, 1830–1870*. Cambridge: Cambridge UP, 1995.

Dye, Ira. "Early American Merchant Seafarers," *Proceedings of the American Philosophical Society*, 102 (1976): 331–60.

Fenn, Elizabeth. *Pox Americana: The Great Smallpox Epidemic of 1775–82*. New York: Hill and Wang, 2001.

Gilje, Paul A. *Liberty on the Waterfront: American Maritime Culture in the Age of Revolution*. Philadelphia: U of Pennsylvania P, 2004.

Heyrman, Christine Leigh. *Commerce and Culture: The Maritime Communities of Colonial Massachusetts, 1690–1750*. New York: Norton, 1984.

Lemisch, Jesse. *Jack Tar vs. John Bull: The Role of New York's Seamen in Precipitating the Revolution*. New York and London: Garland, 1997.

Magra, Christopher P. "Soldiers ... Bred to the Sea: Maritime Marblehead, Massachusetts, and the Origins and Progress of the American Revolution," *New England Quarterly* (2004): 531–62.

Morison, Samuel Eliot. *The Maritime History of Massachusetts, 1783–1860*. Boston, 1921, repr. ed., Boston: Northeastern UP, 1979.

Norling, Lisa. *Captain Ahab Had a Wife: New England Women and the Whalefishery, 1720–1870*. Chapel Hill, NC: U of North Carolina P, 2000.

Pérez-Mallaína, Pablo E. *Spain's Men of the Sea: Daily Life on the Indies Fleet in the Sixteenth Century*, trans. Carla Rahn Phillips. Baltimore: John Hopkins UP, 1998.

Rediker, Marcus. *Between the Devil and the Deep Blue Sea: Merchant Seamen, Pirates and the Anglo-American Maritime World, 1700–1750*. Cambridge: Cambridge UP, 1987.

Rodger, N.A.M. *The Wooden World: An Anatomy of the Georgian Navy*. Annapolis, MD: Naval Institute P, 1986.

Sager, Eric. *Seafaring Labour: The Merchant Marine of Atlantic Canada, 1820–1914*. Montreal and Kingston, ON: McGill-Queen's UP, 1989.

Tagney, Ronald N. *The World Turned Upside Down: Essex County During America's Turbulent Years, 1763–1790*. West Newbury, MA: Essex County History, 1989.

Vickers, Daniel. *Farmers and Fishermen: Two Centuries of Work in Essex County, Massachusetts, 1630–1850*. Chapel Hill, NC: U of North Carolina P, 1994.

Vickers, Daniel. *Young Men and the Sea: Yankee Seafarers in the Age of Sail*, with Vince Walsh. New Haven, CT: Yale UP, 2005.